NATURETRAIL BOOK
of the
Countryside

Usborne Quicklinks

The Usborne Quicklinks Website is packed with thousands of links to all the best websites on the internet. The websites include information, video clips, sounds, games and animations that support and enhance the information in Usborne Internet-linked books.

To visit the recommended websites for the *Naturetrail Book of the Countryside*, go to the Usborne Quicklinks Website at **www.usborne-quicklinks.com** and enter the keyword: **countryside**

When using the internet please follow the internet safety guidelines displayed on the Usborne Quicklinks Website.

The recommended websites in Usborne Quicklinks are regularly reviewed and updated, but Usborne Publishing Ltd. is not responsible for the content or availability of any website other than its own. We recommend that children are supervised while using the internet.

NATURETRAIL BOOK
of the
Countryside

Illustrated by
Brin Edwards, Trevor Boyer,
Ian McNee and Ian Jackson

Consultants: Derek Niemann,
Derek Patch, Tree Advice Trust,
and Dr Mark A. Spencer

CONTENTS

Exploring the countryside

When you are and about in the countryside, there is an amazing amount to see. An ordinary walk can turn into an adventure – especially if you discover something you've never seen before. If you are very lucky, you might even spot something really rare.

This book will tell you where and when to look, and help you to identify many of the most common birds, trees and wild flowers, as well as revealing all sorts of fascinating information about them.

A fieldfare perched on
a hawthorn bush

Birdwatching

Birds are everywhere

If you look out of a window, and look for long enough, you're sure to see a bird – even if you're in the middle of a busy city, or just looking out of a garden window. Once you start looking, it'll be hard not to see them. There are over 10,000 types, or species, of bird in the world, with new ones being discovered all the time. And you can see over 1,000 of them in Europe.

Look for blue tits, dangling like mini-acrobats on the tips of branches.

Begin at home

You don't need to go far to see exciting or exotic-looking birds. You can begin in local streets and gardens, where you might see anything from flocks of boldly painted goldfinches to summer swallows, swooping across the sky. All you need are your eyes, your ears and a little bit of patience.

If you see a little bird with a grey-brown body and a bright red breast, it's unmistakably a robin.

Sparrows flit by in a flash of whirring wings.

The secret lives of birds

Birds have dramatic and amazing lives. Cuckoos, for example, lay their eggs in other birds' nests, and leave other birds to bring up their young. The first thing a cuckoo chick does is to push other chicks from the nest.

Blackbirds are easy to spot, with their glossy feathers and bright beaks.

Drab little dunnocks lurk in bushes, creeping along with mouse-like shuffles to attract as little attention as possible. But, if you catch two rival males together in spring, you'll see them performing strange "wing-waving" displays, flicking up their wings as a sign of aggression and calling loudly.

The more you look at birds, the more fascinating they become. You've started birdwatching the minute you've started to enjoy watching birds.

Chaffinches are colourful little birds. Listen for their "*pink-pink*" calls.

You'll need to look down to see a dunnock, creeping about in the undergrowth.

Willow warbler

Garden
warbler

Sedge warbler

There are lots of species
of birds called warblers
which look pretty much
identical. Before you try
to tell one warbler from
another, learn to spot
easy-to-identify birds,
like the ones below.

Great tit

Magpie

Starting to spot

One of the brilliant things about birds is that
there are so many different species. For the
beginner birdwatcher this might seem a bit
scary, but there is a way around it – just start
off with the easy ones. Being able to tell the
most basic birds apart is a good start. You
probably know many more birds than you
think. Try writing down all the birds you
recognize and see how many you get.

Time to identify

In order to discover the names of new birds,
you'll need an identification guide, also called a
field guide. These are books packed with pictures
of birds and tips for identifying them. They are
also the key to a whole new
world of knowledge. Once you know a bird's
name, you can find out everything else about it
– where it lives, what it sounds like, where it
nests and what it likes for breakfast.

There are lots of field guides to choose from.
Illustrated guides are often better than those with
photographs, as illustrations can show what a
bird looks like more clearly. To find out how good
a guide is, look up a bird you know and see if
you recognize it. The best guides will also have
more than one illustration of the same species.
This is because even birds of the same species have
different colours and patterns on their feathers.

Changing feathers

Taken together, a bird's feathers are known as its plumage. Males can have a different plumage from females and young birds (juveniles) can look different from adults. This is especially true for large birds, such as gulls, which can take several years to grow their adult plumage. And, just to make things even more complicated, some birds change their plumage twice a year.

But, there are ways of using your field guide that will make identifying birds a doddle (well, almost). It's to do with knowing how field guides are set out and being able to identify birds by their beaks. Find out more on the next page...

Here you can see the difference between a juvenile and an adult robin.

Adult   Juvenile

This shows the difference between black-headed gulls in summer and winter.

Summer

Winter

Compare the colouring on this male and female blackbird.

Male

Female

This ptarmigan is halfway through its plumage change. It's changing from its brown summer feathers to its white winter ones, which allow it to blend in against the snow.

These pages from a field guide show members of two bird families – warblers and finches.

Spend time flicking through your field guide, getting familiar with bird families. It'll be a great help if you ever want to look up a bird in a hurry.

Once you're on the "owl" page of your field guide, you'll be able to identify this barn owl by its round, white face.

Using bird field guides

Most field guides show birds in roughly the same order. They start off with water birds, then move onto meat-eating birds, called birds of prey, and end up with seed-eating birds such as sparrows. You'll see headings along the way, such as "ducks", "gulls", "owls" or "thrushes", that group different birds together. These groups are called "families" and contain birds that are more closely related to each other.

This makes your life a lot easier. Imagine you're out birdwatching and you see a bird with a big face, big eyes and a hooked beak. If you already know it's an owl, you can just turn to the "owl" section of your field guide to find out which kind of owl it is, rather than trawling through the whole book.

Birds and their beaks

But suppose you're looking at a bird you've never seen before and you've no idea which family it belongs to. What do you do then? That's when you look at its beak, or bill.

Birds in the same family generally feed on similar food in a similar way. This means they usually have the same shape beak. While a bird's plumage can change with its age and the seasons, you can always tell a bird by its beak.

FANTASTIC FACT

The longest beak record goes to the Australian pelican. Their beaks can be up to 45cm (18in) long. They can hold more food in their beaks than in their bellies.

Chaffinch

Finches have strong, chunky beaks for cracking open the hard shells of nuts and seeds.

Whimbrel

Waders (shore birds) have narrow bills for searching for food in soft mud and sandy shores.

Mute swan

Swans, ducks and geese dabble for plants and tiny animals with their flattish bills.

Kestrel

Birds of prey, such as kestrels, eagles and hawks, use their hooked beaks for tearing strips of meat.

Grey heron

Herons, storks, grebes, cranes and terns have straight, dagger-shaped bills for catching fish.

Blackbird

The thrush family have general-purpose shaped beaks for a mixed diet of fruit, insects and worms.

13

KEY QUESTIONS...

...to help you identify mystery birds. Ask:

1. What size is it? Try and compare it to a bird you know.

2. What shape is it?

3. What colours are its feathers, beak and legs? Are there any striking markings?

4. How does it behave?

5. What's its call or song like?

Being a bird detective

If you're out in a field, or looking through a window, and you spot a mystery bird, the first thing to remember is to keep looking at it. (Don't reach for your field guide in a mad panic). If the bird flies away and you can't remember what it looked like, then you've scuppered your chances of ever finding out what it was. So, instead, keep your eye firmly on it and, like a detective, ask yourself questions as you look.

Then, with your answers in mind, flick through your field guide to find out your mystery bird.

Coots

Mute swans

Duck landing

Female mallard

Male mallard

Mystery bird

14

Making notes

Many birdwatchers carry notebooks with them to make sure they get down all the details. That way, they won't forget any vital info when they try to look up a bird later on.

As well as noting down what a bird looks like, you should also mention the date, time and place where you saw it. This will help you work out what it is. Some birds are only found in a particular type of place, or habitat, such as woods or moors. The time of year is important too, as birds come and go with the seasons.

HANDY HINTS
When you're watching birds, don't just study their appearance. Look at what they're *doing*. Note down how the bird moves and feeds, whether it's on its own or with others, or if it's out in the open or hiding in bushes.

Mystery bird?   April 6th 10.30am
                  Big Lake
          Size - smaller than a swan but
                 bigger than a coot

swan   ?   coot

Shape - Typical duck shape!

Markings -
          black head with
yellow eyes   purple gloss
          droopy crest

Behaviour - Diving for food in shallow water

Call - Making quiet, low whistles

Conclusion -
It's a MALE TUFTED DUCK

This is called upending.

For more information on sketching birds, turn over the page.

Birds' bits and pieces

Each part of a bird has a special name. These words often pop up in field guides and can come in handy when you're trying to describe a bird in detail. For example, you can talk about a goldfinch having a black, white and red head. But if you want to be more specific – and scientific – you should say it has a red forehead, black crown and white ear coverts.

See the picture below for more bird-words, and try to keep them in mind when taking notes.

Wing bars

Secondary feathers

Primary feathers

You can see the wing markings on this flying goldfinch, along with its long primary feathers and shorter secondaries.

This shows the markings of a goldfinch.

Forehead
Crown
Beak or bill
Ear coverts
Nape
Throat
Back
Breast
Wing
Belly
Rump
Flank
Tail

FEATHERY FACT

Birds' feathers are made from a substance called keratin – which is what your nails and hair are made from too.

Simple sketching

Some birdwatchers do simple sketches, and then add their notes around them. You don't have to be good at drawing to do this, and it can be quicker too, as all you have to do is point to the colours and markings.

Here's a step-by-step to doing a quick field sketch:

1. Draw two circles for a head and body.

2. Add a beak, neck, tail and legs.

3. Add details of feathers.

Add wings in order to sketch a bird in flight.

Mystery bird

Seen: 15th April
Clear blue sky. Sitting on telegraph wire.

Red patches

Blue

White on belly

Forked tail

Must have been a swallow

But if you *really* don't want to draw, then don't worry about it. Notes by themselves are just fine. You can also use signs, instead of writing out whole words, to save you time. Look at the pad on the right for some examples.

♂ = MALE
♀ = FEMALE
JUV = JUVENILE/YOUNG (BIRD NOT IN ADULT FEATHERS)
✳ = NEST
C10 = ABOUT TEN (WHEN TALKING ABOUT NUMBERS OF BIRDS)

Winter is the best time to learn bird calls, when few birds are singing and there are fewer leaves on the trees, so birds are easier to see. Listen out for the birds below:

Blue tit
Where: woods
Call: *tsee-tsee-tsee*

Chaffinch
Where: woods & gardens
Call: *pink-pink*

Jackdaw
Where: fields
Call: *jack*

Grey heron
Where: lakes & ponds
Call: *frank* (when flying)

Calls and songs

You'll often hear a bird before you see it. Or you'll hear a bird and see nothing at all, if it's flying high or hiding in the undergrowth. This is where knowing a bird by its call or song comes in very handy. All birds use calls to communicate with each other, and you'll hear these throughout the year. Songs are more complicated, tuneful sounds and birds usually only sing in spring.

A robin on its song perch. Robins are one of the few birds that sing all year round.

Bird talk

To learn bird sounds, begin by trying to find the bird that's making a noise. Next time you'll connect up the bird and the sound in your head. To help make bird sounds clearer, cup your ears as you listen.

Birds have different calls to mean different things, such as alarm calls to signal danger, or calls to make contact with other birds. Watch what birds are doing as they call, to see if you can work out what their different calls mean.

Songsters and tricksters

In spring, especially at dawn and dusk, the air suddenly comes alive with birdsong. Male birds sing to attract females and to warn other birds away from their territory – the area where they nest and feed. Listen out for each new species as it comes into song.

There's no way around the fact that learning bird songs can take ages. It's like grasping a whole new language. What's worse is that some birds seem as if they're out to trick you on purpose. Listen carefully and you'll hear blackbirds impersonating alarm clocks, song thrushes imitating lawnmowers and starlings sounding like anything from buzzards to sheep and frogs.

If you hear a starling singing, you might think it's your telephone.

This list shows some of the first birds to come into song in spring. Make a list of your own and add to it.

My spring bird list:

Song thrush
1st heard: Feb 6th
Sings – very loudly!
Short, varied phrases,
repeated 2-4 times.

Great tit
1st heard: Feb 26th
Sings – a loud and
rhythmic phrase:
tea-cher, tea-cher, tea-cher.

Blackbird
1st heard: Mar 7th
Sings – a simple series
of phrases of 2-4 fluty
notes, separated by pauses.

Chiffchaff
1st heard: Mar 25th
Sings—its name, but in a
funny order: chiff-chaff,
chaff-chiff, chaff-chiff-chiff.

Cuckoo
1st heard: Apr 18th
Sings – a far-carrying
"cuc-oo, cuc-oo". The
female has a bubbling trill.

Flying high

One of the best things about birdwatching is watching birds fly. With the help of light, hollow bones, powerful muscles and a covering of feathers, birds achieve what humans can only dream of... the ability to soar, dive, flap and zoom across the sky. Watching them can give a sense of wonder, whether it's the rapid whirring wingbeats of a sparrow, or the steep power dive of a falcon, hunting on the wing.

Jay feather

Magnified view

Barbule with hooks   Barb   Shaft

Flight styles

As you watch birds fly you'll notice that different kinds of birds fly in different ways. There are four main types of flight to look out for: flapping, gliding, soaring and hovering.
In *flapping flight*, a bird beats its wings up and down. Some birds, such as herons, flap their huge wings very slowly, while others, such as kingfishers, flap their wings so fast all you can see is a blur of blue.

Here you can see the flapping flight of a coal tit. Sparrows, tits, thrushes and warblers all have flapping flight.

20

In *gliding flight*, a bird holds out its wings stiffly to catch air currents. This allows it to stay in the air for a long time without having to waste energy flapping.

To achieve *soaring flight*, a bird holds its wings in the same way, but uses up-currents of warm air to gain height, so that it spirals upwards through the sky.

Only a very few birds use *hovering flight*, which allows them to hover in the air in one spot. They do this by angling their bodies and flapping their wings very quickly.

A kittiwake gliding

A kestrel hovering

Flight patterns

If you watch birds flying, you'll see they make a pattern in the air as they fly. This is called a flight path. Knowing a bird's flight path will help you to identify it, even if it's just a speck in the sky.

Buzzard

A buzzard's flight path - gliding, then soaring, up and up...

Great spotted woodpecker

A woodpecker's flight path – flapping, then gliding, which makes a wavy pattern.

Mallard

A mallard's flight path – mad, panicky flapping to get into the air, then fast and straight across the sky.

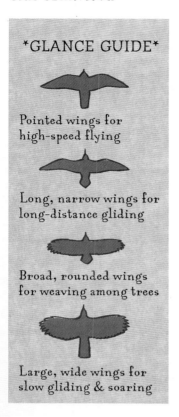

Pointed wings for
high-speed flying

Long, narrow wings for
long-distance gliding

Broad, rounded wings
for weaving among trees

Large, wide wings for
slow gliding & soaring

Birds in flight

The shape of a bird's wing tells a story – about its way of life. Birds that spend most of their time in the air, such as swifts, swallows and falcons, have long, narrow wings. As a rule, the more pointed the wing, the faster the bird. Wide wings are for gliding and soaring at slow speeds, and birds that hunt in open spaces have the widest wings of all. Woodland birds have shorter wings for weaving among trees.

To identify birds in flight, look at the shape of the tail and wing, and for any noticeable markings, such as wing bars and patches of white. Note down whether a bird's neck is long or short, and if its feet stick out behind its tail.

Woods and gardens
If you live in the countryside, you'll have a chance of seeing all these birds from your window. Magpies, with their very long tails, are one of the easiest to spot.

Chaffinch

Blackbird

Great spotted
woodpecker

Jay

Magpie

Towns and cities

There are a surprising number of birds to see in towns. Pigeons rule the ground, but look up to catch a glimpse of gulls and crows – and, if you're lucky, a sparrowhawk.

House sparrow

Swift

Carrion crow

Black-headed gull

Sparrowhawk

Ponds, lakes and rivers

You can hear ducks, geese and swans as they fly, as well as see them – listen for their deep wingbeats. Herons are easy to spot too, with their huge wingspan and long legs.

Kingfisher

Mallard

Brent goose

Mute swan

Grey heron

FANTASTIC FACT

No one is sure how birds find their way on long migrations. It is thought they use the position of the sun and the stars and the earth's magnetic field to guide them.

Winging it

Many of the birds you see around you have come from far and wide. The swallow that flits across our summer skies would fit into the palm of your hand and weighs less than a bar of chocolate. But it has flown thousands of miles to reach Europe. Birds make these amazing journeys twice every year, to find food or breeding sites, where they can nest and bring up their young. This is called migration and the birds are known as migrants.

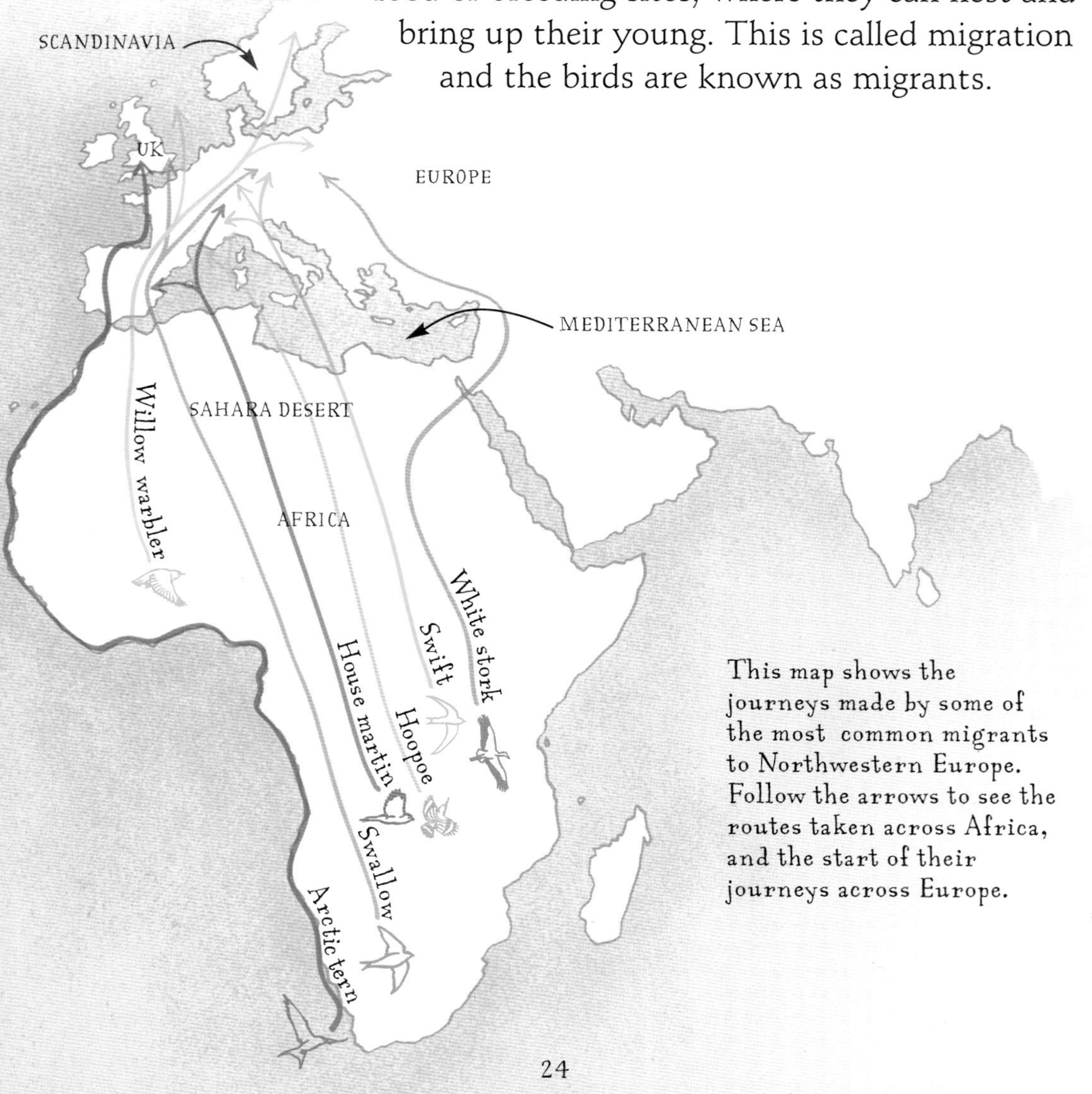

SCANDINAVIA
UK
EUROPE
MEDITERRANEAN SEA
SAHARA DESERT
AFRICA
Willow warbler
White stork
Swift
Hoopoe
House martin
Swallow
Arctic tern

This map shows the journeys made by some of the most common migrants to Northwestern Europe. Follow the arrows to see the routes taken across Africa, and the start of their journeys across Europe.

Arctic terns make one of the longest journeys. They winter in the Antarctic and some then fly all the way to the Arctic for the summer.

House martins look similar to swallows but have a white rump and a shorter tail, and are more likely to be seen in towns and cities. They arrive in Europe between mid-April and early May.

Swifts are one of the last summer migrants, arriving in mid-May. Look for them in the sky flying after insects, and listen out for their screaming cries.

Willow warblers are our commonest migrants. They arrive from mid-April to mid-May and can be seen flitting through trees.

Hoopoes are astonishingly hardy migrants. They fly over both the Sahara and the Alps, arriving in Europe in the spring. They have very broad, black and white wings, and a floppy, moth-like flight.

White storks arrive from mid-March to April. They have a gliding, soaring flight, relying on up-currents of warm air to help them on their journey.

Swallows arrive from late March onwards and stay till late summer. You can see them on telegraph wires as they gather together for the journey back.

New arrivals

Most summer migrants arrive in Europe in April or May. This makes spring an exciting time for birdwatching, as you can look out for new visitors. You could keep a record of the first and last dates you see birds through the year. Make a note of the weather too, to see if it affects when birds arrive or leave.

May 17th
Weather warm & dry.
First swifts arrive from the south, spotted zooming around the rooftops.

Spring displays

As well as watching out for migrant birds, spring is also the best time to see birds showing off to each other. In order to win mates and territories to nest in, male birds sing their hearts out and make fascinating flight and feather displays. Male black grouse, for example, display together in an area known as a "lek" in order to win over admiring females.

FIGHTING FACT

Birds solve arguments in different ways. Male coots fight for females with noisy kicks, while puffins strike each other with their claws.

At dawn, the male black grouse strut around, and fan out their tail feathers.

They make "sneezing" calls and act out show fights, as females look on.

Each female then chooses the male that impresses her most.

Because male birds usually do the displaying, they tend to have more colourful feathers than the females. So if you're wondering which is a male and which is a female in a pair, you'll know the male by his brighter plumage.

You can see the gleaming red and blue feathers on this male pheasant. The females, by contrast, are a dull brown.

Songflight

Birds that live in open spaces take to the air to display, so they can be seen for miles around. Some birds combine flight displays with song. This is known as a songflight.

Lapwing songflight

If you are in the countryside, look out for the mad songflight of lapwings – one of the more unusual sights of spring. They display above fields, moors and marshes, flapping crazily into the sky and rocking from side to side. Then they tumble down again, crying *"pee-wit"* as they go.

Skylark songflight

The skylark's songflight is perhaps one of the best known. The male bird rises high into the air, then hovers on fluttering wings before parachuting back down to the ground. It sings continuously in the air, with a liquid, warbling song.

Snipe use a different way of claiming nesting sites. They fly high in the air, spread out their stiff tail feathers and dive steeply. The tail feathers vibrate to make a loud humming noise that says, "Keep out! This area's mine!"

Many writers have been inspired by the skylark's song. The lines below are by the famous poet, William Wordsworth.

TO A SKYLARK

UP with me! up with me into the clouds!
For thy song, Lark, is strong;
Up with me, up with me into the clouds!
Singing, singing,
With clouds and sky about thee ringing,
Lift me, guide me till I find
That spot which seems so to thy mind!

An osprey
collecting
nesting materials

HANDY HINTS

Look out for these
clues to spot nest sites:

*Birds singing from
the same perch
every day to
mark their
nest site

*Birds flying
and fro,
carrying
materials
for nest-building

*Birds with
droppings in
their beaks,
cleaning out their nests

*Broken eggshells
on the ground – a
sign that chicks
have just hatched.

The nesting season

Once the male bird has strutted and sung and paraded himself as much as he can, with any luck he will have won a mate. Then the pair have no time to waste – they must quickly build a nest, lay their eggs and raise their young. You may be lucky enough to see birds frantically flitting to and fro, searching for a good nesting spot, and then gathering material for the nest.

But, once the eggs are laid, nesting sites become trickier to spot. It is usually the female birds that sit on the eggs, and they tend to have dull plumage and markings, to match their backgrounds. This makes them hard to see. Blending into the background like this is known as camouflage. It helps birds stay hidden from other animals that could be after their eggs.

This reed warbler is hard
to see in her nest.

Where birds nest

In the countryside, birds nest in many different places. Look out for rooks' nests in the tops of trees and swans' nests in rivers and lakes. If you walk along a river, you might be close to a kingfisher's nest without knowing it. They dig tunnels in river banks to lay their eggs.

In the city, look for crows flying up to their nests on top of church towers, sparrows flitting into crevices in old walls, or gulls simply nesting on window ledges.

Guillemots nest on cliff ledges and lay pointed eggs. If knocked, the eggs roll in circles, rather than off the cliff.

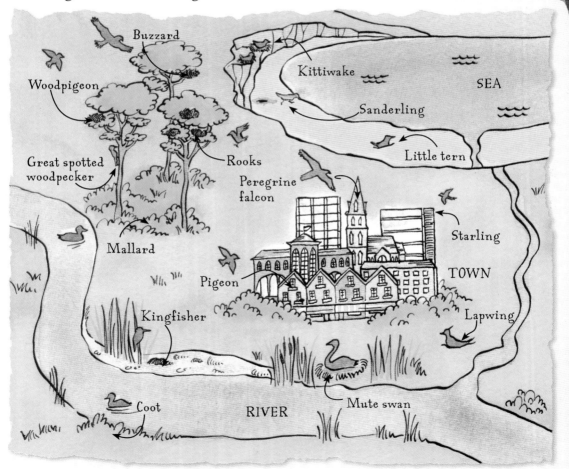

Buzzard

Woodpigeon

Kittiwake

SEA

Sanderling

Great spotted woodpecker

Rooks

Little tern

Peregrine falcon

Starling

Mallard

TOWN

Pigeon

Kingfisher

Lapwing

Coot

RIVER

Mute swan

This swallow is bringing food to its young. The bright red lining of their mouths shows the parents where to drop food.

HANDY HINTS

Try watching a nest site to record the number of visits parent birds make over an hour. You can do this by drawing a clock face and labelling every five minutes, in the way shown below. Then draw a line to mark each visit.

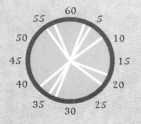

Hatching out

Birds sit on their eggs for anything from two weeks to 80 days. Larger birds usually lay the eggs that take longer to hatch. You shouldn't get too close to nesting birds: if you disturb the parents they may abandon their eggs. But, once the eggs have hatched, the fun begins – you can watch, and listen, from a safe distance.

Chicks in the nest are known as nestlings. You might hear their cheeping noises as they call for food. You can also watch the parents flying to and from the nest to feed their hungry young. Some birds make hundreds of trips. Great tits have been known to visit their nests over 600 times a day with insects.

Growing feathers

Nestlings in trees are usually born without any feathers at all, and are completely dependent on their parents. Their first feathers are soft and downy and are designed for warmth. It is only once they grow stiffer feathers that they are able to leave the nest and fly. Robins, for example, take around thirteen days to grow their flight feathers. Then their parents feed them for three more weeks while they learn to fly well. After that, they're left to fend for themselves.

A robin chick at day 1, naked and blind.

A robin chick at day 3, with its first feathers.

A robin chick at day 13, with flight feathers.

Fast learners

While some birds are born as blind pink blobs, others emerge from their eggs covered in downy feathers and ready to take care of themselves. These birds are usually ones that have been born on the ground or in floating nests on water, such as ducklings and cygnets (baby swans). They need to be active and alert, as they are very vulnerable to attack.

Mallards can swim the day they hatch, and know to dive to escape from danger.

At five days old, an oystercatcher can already run well and practice catching insects.

Shelducks quickly copy their parents and learn to sift food from the water.

31

A travelling circus

It's one of the most spectacular shows in Europe. It features a dazzling array of singers, sky divers, dancers and acrobats. The performers come from all over the world – from Scandinavia, Russia and even South Africa. And where is this amazing spectacle? It all takes place in back gardens and local parks. The performers are garden birds – some of the most fascinating creatures on the planet.

Garden birds are ideal birds to study as you'll get to see the same birds over and over again. You'll get to know what they look like, and what they do. But be prepared for a few surprises.

This is a nuthatch. You can tell as it's the only bird to walk headfirst down bird feeders.

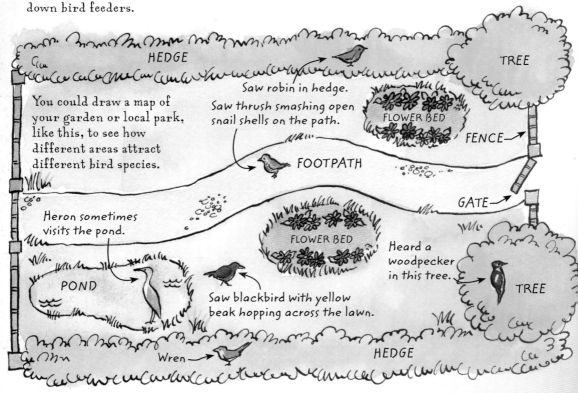

HEDGE

TREE

Saw robin in hedge.
Saw thrush smashing open snail shells on the path.

FLOWER BED

You could draw a map of your garden or local park, like this, to see how different areas attract different bird species.

FENCE →

FOOTPATH

GATE →

Heron sometimes visits the pond.

FLOWER BED

Heard a woodpecker in this tree.

POND

TREE

Saw blackbird with yellow beak hopping across the lawn.

Wren →

HEDGE

Expect the unexpected

You might see a robin merrily singing from his perch every day. But what if another robin lands on his branch? Both birds disappear in a flurry of wings – rolling over on the ground – then flapping up together in the air. The intruder will be lucky to get away. Robins will fight fiercely to defend their territory.

Many thrushes, such as blackbirds, will squabble over mates, or viciously attack each other for a piece of food. But they do have good table manners: watch thrushes after they've eaten and you'll often see them fly up to a fence, wipe one side of their beaks on the fence, and then the other.

If you watch garden birds day in, day out, you'll soon glimpse another side to the secret lives of birds.

RED ALERT

The colour red makes robins aggressive. They may attack anything even slightly red – from a pile of autumn leaves to a bushy ginger beard.

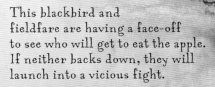

This blackbird and fieldfare are having a face-off to see who will get to eat the apple. If neither backs down, they will launch into a vicious fight.

Instead of buying bird food, you could make a bird cake, using nuts, cake crumbs, oatmeal and dried fruit. Just follow the steps below.

1. Put 500g (1lb) of the ingredients into a heat-resistant bowl.

2. Melt 250g (0.5lb) of solid fat in a saucepan at a low heat. Then carefully pour the fat over the mixture, and leave it to set.

3. Turn the cake out when it's cold and put it out in the garden. Then watch the birds peck away at it.

Feed the birds

The simplest way to encourage birds to come to your garden is to feed them. Birds will eat all sorts of food – from nuts and fruit, to bacon bits and cheese. Some birds search for food on the ground, while others feed on branches of trees, so it's important to leave food out at different levels. You could wedge lumps of cheese into the bark of trees, leave seeds and nuts out on a bird table, or scatter pieces of fruit on the ground.

These birds quickly eat up the bird food scattered on the ground. Can you tell which birds they are? *

It's especially important to leave out food in winter, when birds' natural sources of food are scarce. By December, fruits will have been eaten, insects are hiding away and the ground may have frozen over. Birds need lots of energy at this time, to help them to survive the cold winter nights.

*Male and female blackbird, and five greenfinches.

How to make a bird feeder

To make a bird feeder of your own, you will need a pencil, some scissors, some string and a plastic milk carton.

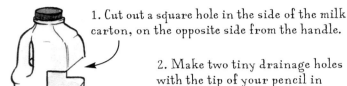

1. Cut out a square hole in the side of the milk carton, on the opposite side from the handle.

2. Make two tiny drainage holes with the tip of your pencil in the base.

3. Push a pencil through the carton to make a perch.

4. Fill the feeder with seeds. Then use the string to hang the feeder from a tree, a washing line or a bird table.

A room with a view

If you don't have a garden, you can set up a feeding station on a sheltered windowsill. You could use a window box as a feeding area. Fill it almost to the top with soil, and put the food on the surface.

HANDY HINTS

Thread peanuts in their shells on thin string, and hang them up in winter. Don't put them out in spring or summer though, as young birds can choke on them.

BIRD MENU

Do put out:

Oats
Seeds
Soaked raisins
Cheese
Cooked rice
- unsalted, as birds can't process salt

Bread
- only in winter, as young birds choke on it

~

Don't put out:

Salted peanuts
Roasted peanuts
Milk
- birds can't digest it

Cooked porridge
- it glues birds' beaks together

All these plants make good bird food.

Rowan

Ivy

Shepherd's purse

Wild grasses

Hawthorn

Thistle

Bird gardens

Trees and bushes in gardens and parks provide food, shelter and nesting sites for birds. In the summer, lots of birds feed off fruit trees, while in the autumn, they visit gardens to pluck berries off bushes. Rowan berries, for example, attract chaffinches and siskins. Weeds, such as thistle and shepherd's purse, are especially popular with finches, which love to eat the seeds.

Thirsty birds

Birds need water too, for drinking and cleaning their feathers. Providing water is especially useful during hot, dry summers and very cold winters, when ponds and streams freeze over. If you have a garden pond, birds will drink and bathe in it. If you don't, a deep plant pot saucer can make an excellent bird bath.

A greenfinch drinks from a garden pond. Doves are the only birds that can gulp down water, so this greenfinch will have to tip back its head to swallow.

Gobbling and guzzling

If you watch birds feed, you'll soon learn what food they like to eat, and how they eat it. Robins pick randomly at berries, starlings feed in large gangs, while one song thrush may viciously attack another to steal its food. Crows bury any extra food they find, disguise the hiding place, and then return later to uncover their stash.

   The more you watch, the more you will learn about the different lives of birds. You could make a feeding chart to keep a record.

This blackbird is about to snap up a redcurrant.

Feeding Chart						
Bird	Insects	Berries	Seeds	Cheese	Apples	Nuts
Blue tit 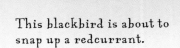	✓	✓	✓	✗	✗	✓
Dunnock	✓	✗	✓	✓	✗	✗
Blackbird	✓	✓	✗	✓	✓	✗

Observations:

Saw a sparrowhawk come in low over the garden hedge and grab a blue tit from the bird feeder. It snatched it up in its claws and flew off with it.

Later found lots of feathers scattered beneath a stump. The sparrowhawk must have plucked it first before eating it.

IN THE TREES

Blue tits and great tits will scrap over food on feeders, but they don't fight when they return to trees. They find food on different parts of the branches.

Great tits search on thicker twigs.

Lighter blue tits can hang from the thinnest, outermost twigs.

Other birds to spot on the feeder:

Long-tailed tit (see p.57)
Nuthatch (see p.57)

Birds to spot beneath the feeder:

Chaffinch (see p.40)
Dunnock (see p.40)
Fieldfare (see p.41)
Wren (see p.40)

On a bird feeder

Bird feeders are home to some of the most acrobatic garden birds. They will give you a great opportunity to see birds close up, and marvel at their gravity-defying antics as they flit, dance and peck at their food. Nuthatches strut down feeders headfirst while blue tits hang upside down on them, grasping on with their feet. Here are some of the birds you might see on your feeder.

Coal tit
11cm/4"
Looks a little like a great tit, but is smaller and less colourful. Olive grey on top, black head and white cheeks. All year round.

Blue tit
11cm/4"
Bright blue, yellow and green bird. It sometimes raises the blue feathers on its head to form a small crest. All year round.

Great tit
14cm/5.5"
The biggest European tit. It will budge blue tits away with a simple squawk. All year round.

Greenfinch
15cm/6"
The clumsy clown of the feeder. Not very acrobatic, but it still gets at the food with its large beak. All year round.

Female

Male

Summer visitors

Summer time can bring many fascinating visitors to your garden or local park. Swifts spend nearly their whole life on the wing: sleeping, eating and mating in the air. The sky is their playground – just watch as they soar gracefully overhead. You can also spot house martins high in the sky. Look for spotted flycatchers diving after insects and swallows flitting closer to the ground.

FANTASTIC FACT

Swifts are one of the few types of birds that sleep on the wing. Before dusk, swifts rise 1,000–2,000m (3,300-6,500ft) to roost in a warmer layer of air. They can hover perfectly still as they sleep.

House martin
13cm/5"
Listen out for its twittering song. Visits farmland, gardens and woodland. April to October.

Redstart
14cm/5.5"
Black face, orange rump and chest. Constantly flicks its bright red tail. Summer visitor to heaths, parks and gardens.

Female

Male

Spotted flycatcher
14cm/5.5"
Sits on branches, and flies out to snap up insects before returning to its perch. Woodland edges. Spring and summer.

Nightingale
17cm/7"
Secretive summer visitor to dense thickets and woodland. Best found by listening out for its song in May and June.

Swift
17cm/7"
Seen high in the sky above towns and countryside. Has a screaming call. May to August.

Swallow
19cm/7.5"
Its long tail feathers help it to be such an expert flyer. Visits farmland and gardens. March to October.

Listen out for a smacking sound and you might find a thrush. They smash snail shells against a stone and then gobble up the juicy insides.

On the ground

As well as looking up to see birds perched in trees or flying through the air, you can also spot lots of birds by looking down. You'll see birds strutting across grassy lawns or nipping around under thickets and bushes. These birds are searching for juicy worms, spiders, slugs and other creepy crawlies to eat. Here are a few of the birds you are likely to spot on the ground.

Wren
9.5cm/3.5"
Can be found in holes and crevices in bushes, looking for spiders and insects to eat. All year round.

Marsh tit
11cm/4"
Drawn to gardens by peanuts and seeds. Particularly fond of sunflower seeds. All year round.

Robin
14cm/5.5"
Swoops down to the ground to catch insects and worms after watching from a perch. All year round.

Dunnock
14.5cm/6"
Rummages in piles of leaves to find spiders, ants and beetles. Constantly flicks its tail and wings. All year round.

Chaffinch
15cm/6"
The flamboyant male has a reddish breast, while the female has a brown breast. All year round.

Female

Male

Starling
22cm/9"
Probes into the ground with its beak to find food. Usually flies in a large flock. All year round.

Juvenile

Adult

Song thrush
23cm/9"
Hops along the grass, and then stands still, as it looks and listens for worms and other creepy crawlies to eat. All year round.

Blackbird
25cm/10"
Bright yellow beak and sleek black body. The female is brown without the eye ring. Listen out for its melodic song. All year round.

Female

Male

Fieldfare
25.5cm/10"
Blue-grey head, brown back and yellow-brown speckled breast. Visits gardens in winter to eat seeds and berries.

Mistle thrush
27cm/11"
Creamy yellow breast with large spots. Moves in long, bouncy hops. All year round.

Collared dove
30cm/12"
Distinctive black collar. Searches the ground for seeds, berries and grain. All year round.

Green woodpecker
32cm/13"
Green upper parts, red crown and moustache. Female has a black moustache. All year round.

Woodpigeon
41cm/16"
Waddles along the ground. Its distinctive call goes "*ru-hoo ru ru-hoo*". All year round.

Magpie
46cm /18"
Black and white body with glossy wings, tinged with blue, and a long tail. Its call goes "*chacker-chacker*". All year round.

FEATHERY FACT
Some birds allow ants to crawl all over them.

They probably do this because a liquid from the ants helps clean their feathers.

These grey herons are squabbling over food in Regent's Park, London.

Rarer visitors

While some birds have made gardens and parks their home, others only ever drop in for a visit, either when food in their usual habitat is running low, or in search of shelter. What birds you see will depend on where you live.

If there are woods near your garden or local park, you might see a goldfinch, while if you live near fields, you may find a jackdaw nesting in your chimney.

Larger birds, like sparrowhawks, are passing visitors. They usually come in search of smaller birds they can snatch up as prey. If you live near a pond or lake, look out for herons hunting for fish.

Rarer birds to spot

Siskin
11cm/4"
Will visit gardens if conifer trees are nearby, or if its usual food has run low. Most commonly seen in winter.

Male

Female

Goldfinch
11cm/4"
Usually lives in fields or woods. May be drawn into gardens by teasels, or by its favourite food - nyjer seeds. All year round.

Blackcap
13cm/5"
Most often seen in summer, but will also visit bird tables in winter. Found in areas with trees or shrubs.

Female   Male

Brambling
15cm/6"
Lives in woodland, but visits gardens in winter, often in flocks. Male's head is greyish-black in winter.

Female

Male

Bullfinch
15cm/6"
A very secretive bird that usually lives in woodland. Will sometimes eat from garden feeders.

Female

Male

Waxwing
17cm/7"
Pinkish-brown bird, with black eye patches. A rare winter visitor. Usually lives in woods, but will also visit gardens and parks to eat berries.

Pied & white wagtail
18cm/7"
Searches the ground for food. Its wagging tail never stops. White wagtail is found in Europe. Pied wagtail only in Britain.

Pied wagtail   White wagtail

Cuckoo
30cm/12"
Looks similar to a sparrowhawk, with its sleek body, long tail and pointed wings. Summer visitor all over Europe.

Juvenile

Adult

Jackdaw
33cm/13"
Small black crow with a grey neck. Seen in pairs or groups. Breeds in gardens with fields nearby. All year round.

This blue tit is collecting dog hair for the soft lining of its nest.

HANDY HINTS

Nest boxes with different sized holes attract different birds:

Small: 25mm/1"
Bird: blue tit

Medium: 32mm/1.3"
Bird: house sparrow

Large: 45mm/1.8"
Bird: starling

Garden nests

In spring, birds find lots of places to nest in gardens. Some use bushes, trees, ivy-covered walls or sheds. Others, such as house martins and swallows, build their nests under roofs.

Many garden birds will also use nest boxes, as the spread of towns and farms has taken over a lot of their natural nesting spots. If you put a nest box up in your garden, make sure you leave it in a quiet, sheltered place, at least 2m (6.5ft) above the ground. Fix the nest box facing north or east, out of direct sunlight.

Hairy nests

You can help birds to build nests by leaving out materials for them, such as moss, twigs, feathers and wool, which you can hang from fences or trees. Some birds also use human hair to line their nests, which might have inspired this limerick by Edward Lear.

There was an Old Man with a beard,
Who said, "It is just as I feared!
Two Owls and a Hen,
Four Larks and a Wren,
Have all built their nests in my beard!"

44

Inside a nest

In the autumn, when leaves fall from the trees, it's easy to see birds' nests that were hidden in the summer. By now the nests will be empty, and you could collect them for yourself.

Like a detective carefully examining evidence, you can find out a lot about birds by looking at an old nest.

!IMPORTANT!

Some birds make their nests out of mud. If you see a mud nest, don't disturb it. The same birds may return to it next year.

1. First make a note of where the nest is, and how far it is from the ground.

2. Then, wearing gloves, take down the nest, and look inside. You might find interesting things the bird has used to line its nest, such as dog or cat hair or pieces of string.

3. Now you can start to pull different materials out of the nest, using a pair of tweezers.

4. You could stick the nest materials to a piece of card, with all the other data you have gathered.

Birds in urban areas will often use strips of paper and plastic, instead of the more usual grass and leaves.

Leaves

Moss

Twigs →

Grass

How far has it flown?

By looking at what a nest is made of, you can sometimes tell how far a bird must have flown in order to gather the materials.

Mute swans in flight – easy birds to identify with the naked eye.

USING BINS

You'll need to focus a pair of binoculars, or "bins", before you can use them:

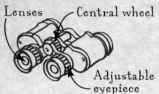

Lenses — Central wheel

Adjustable eyepiece

1. Close your right eye, then turn the left lens with the central wheel until an object comes into focus.

2. Close your left eye and look through the right lens. Make the image appear sharper using the adjustable eyepiece.

3. Don't touch the adjustable eyepiece again, just focus the central wheel when you see birds close up or far away.

Going out and about

There's a whole world of birdwatching beyond your garden or local park, just waiting to be explored. Wear light, warm clothing on birdwatching trips, and keep to dull colours, as that will make you harder to spot. Other than that, all you need is your field guide, pen and paper, and your wits.

Looking closer

Birds have good eyesight and hearing and are always on the look out for danger. So don't be surprised if you have trouble getting close to them. To avoid looking at dots in the distance, try and get your hands on a pair of binoculars.

You'll find they come in different sizes, such as 8x30 or 10x40. The first number is the magnification power: "8", for example, allows you to see a bird 8 times closer, and the second number refers to the amount of light the lenses let in. The higher the second number, the better the binoculars in low light. But they are also bigger and harder to carry, so you need to think about this when choosing them.

A mute swan as seen through binoculars. Being able to see the extra detail makes the bird even easier to identify.

46

Stalking birds

It takes a bit of practice to watch birds through binoculars, and to be able to follow a bird's flight across the sky. It's often easier to find a bird, then raise the binoculars to your eyes, rather than looking for birds with your binoculars first. It also helps to keep the sun behind you, as most birds look black against a bright sky.

Even with binoculars, you need to be careful not to scare birds away. Try to camouflage your shape by standing in front of or behind a tree. Never break cover by looking over a bush or a hedge – peer around it instead. If there's no cover in sight, just keep as still and quiet as you can.

HANDY HINTS

Be careful not to trespass across other people's land, so make sure you have permission wherever you go. Don't go out alone and let an adult know where you are.

The dotted line shows an ideal stalking route to get close to birds.

Check birds at intervals as you stalk. If they seem alarmed, go no closer.

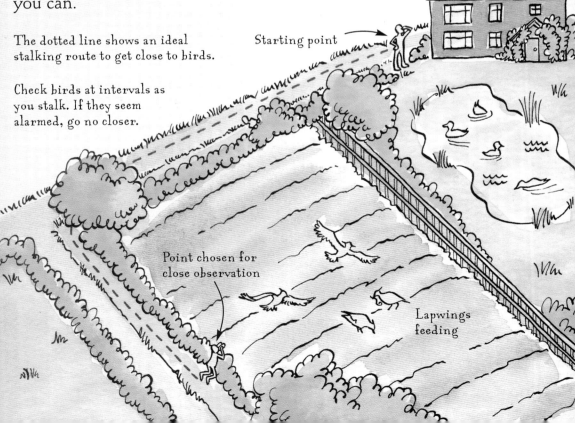

Starting point

Point chosen for close observation

Lapwings feeding

Where to look

The best places to go birdwatching are areas that offer birds lots of food and shelter. As a rule, the more varied the habitat, the more bird species you're likely to see. For this reason, places where two habitats meet, such as where woodland gives way to farmland, or where a river meets the sea, are often brilliant birdwatching sites.

Nature reserves

If you're not sure where to go, or if you've been out on a few trips and not seen many birds, try to visit your nearest nature reserve.

These areas are managed to create the best conditions for wildlife and attract as many species as possible. There are usually paths to follow and signs showing which birds to look out for. Some nature reserves also have huts, known as hides, which provide birdwatchers with shelter from bad weather and great views of birds. Some hides will also have telescopes so you can get amazing close-ups.

This is a view of a hide in a nature reserve in Norfolk, UK. There are whooper and Bewick's swans, coots, mallards and pochards.

Picky habits

As you visit different areas, you'll notice that while some birds, such as herring gulls, seem to be able to live anywhere and eat lots of different things, others are much more picky about where they live. For example, you'll only ever see crossbills where there are pine trees, as they only eat pine shoots, buds and seeds, while bitterns will only ever breed in large, wet reedbeds.

BIZARRE BEAKS
Crossbills are very strange looking birds – the tips of their beaks cross over. They use them to prise apart the scales on fir cones so they can get at the seeds inside.

Birds like crossbills and bitterns are known as specialists. They tend to be rarer than birds that have adapted to live anywhere, especially if their habitat is under threat from farming, building or pollution. But rare birds are worth the effort – you'll get a thrill of excitement even if you just catch a glimpse of one. The key is to go birdwatching in as many different habitats as possible, so you're always discovering new birds. Here are some rare birds to look out for.

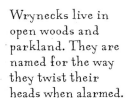

Wrynecks live in open woods and parkland. They are named for the way they twist their heads when alarmed.

Bitterns only breed in reedbeds, but spend winter in well-vegetated marshes and in reeds around lakes.

Ptarmigans live on high mountain slopes, only coming below the heather line in very harsh winters.

Capercaillies are found only in old conifer woods. They are becoming very rare as much forest land is being cleared.

Bird clues

Sometimes you may not be able to see any birds, but it doesn't mean they're not there. Keep your eyes peeled for other clues, such as feathers, footprints and the remains of meals.

Hazelnut eaten by a woodpecker

Look for nibbled nuts and pine cones, although these may have been eaten by small mammals.

Barn owl feather

Collect clean, undamaged feathers to build up a good collection.

Gull pellet

Look out for pellets that birds have coughed up at feeding and nesting sites.

You're most likely to find feathers from early-spring to late-summer when birds are replacing their feathers, in a process known as moulting. You'll notice there are several different types, such as tail, wing and body feathers. Try to identify which bird they're from. You can then stick the feathers in a book.

Date:
6th September

Where found:
beach

Bird:
oystercatcher

Make two cuts in the page, 6mm apart, then thread the feather through.

Looking at pellets

Many birds swallow their food whole, then cough up the parts they can't digest, such as bones, fur, feathers and insect parts. It's hard to tell what's in most bird pellets, but by looking at owl pellets you can get an idea of what they've eaten. They can't digest bones, so their pellets may contain all the parts of a skeleton.

Feet and tracks

Birds' tracks are usually hard to find because birds are light-footed and spend little time on the ground. But you can look for tracks in snow, mud or sand. Notice the size and shape of any you find, and if the footprints are together (paired) or one after the other (alternate). Birds that walk or run make alternate tracks, and birds that hop make paired ones.

A blackbird hops, so it makes paired tracks.

A pigeon leaves zig-zag alternate tracks.

A pheasant makes a straight line of alternate tracks.

EXAMINING OWL PELLETS

1. Soak the pellet in disinfected water for an hour. Put it on newspaper, then prise it apart with sticks or needles.

2. Using tweezers, pick out tiny bones and teeth, and remove any feathers or fur.

3. Clean each part with a fine brush.

4. Try to identify any jaws, skulls or insect shells with a magnifying glass.

5. Keep your finds in boxes or stick them onto cardboard with glue & label them. Always wash your hands afterwards.

51

Keeping a bird diary

At the end of a birdwatching trip, even if it's just a day in the park, you can write up your notes in a bird diary, so you have a permanent record of all that you've seen.

You can stick photos, maps and feathers in your bird diary.

Robin

Curlew feather

Jay sketch

Put month & date here

3rd SEPTEMBER IN THE GARDEN
WEATHER - SUNNY AND WINDY

BIRD	HOW MANY?	WHERE?
BLUE TIT	1	ON FEEDER
HERRING GULL	5	IN SKY
JAY	1	ON GROUND

OBSERVATIONS:
Saw jay picking up acorns from the ground. It ate about five and must have been stuffing them in the food pouch in its throat. It then flew off with one acorn still in its beak. It was probably going to bury the acorns in the ground as a food store for later.

Stick in sketches too

Add bird observations

HANDY HINTS

Look up your local county bird recorder on the Internet. You can then send them your bird records, along with any sightings of rare birds.

Making records

A diary is like a detective's notebook. If you add to it year after year, noting down the birds you see, you will have a record of how the birdlife changes with the seasons. You'll also notice which birds are flourishing, and which are not. You could try to work out why some birds might be getting rarer. It could be because their habitat is getting smaller, or because of wider issues, such as global warming.

A flock of house martins gather together for their journey back to Africa.

Bird casebook

Your bird diary is also your key to unravelling the mysterious lives of birds. If house martins nest near your home, for example, you might note down what date in spring you first see them swooping overhead. Watch to see when they start collecting mud to build their nests, and how often they visit their young. Then look out for the last ones in the sky as they return to Africa.

As you read back through your diary, you'll be able to build up a picture of birds' lives.

You could collect together your diary notes about one species of bird, then put your notes on a separate card.

COUNTING FLOCKS

To record migrating birds, you need to be able to work out flock sizes. First, count a small number of birds, such as ten. Then estimate roughly how many groups of ten are in the whole flock and multiply that number by ten.

HOUSE MARTINS

DATE	WEATHER	DETAILS
23rd April	Gloomy, cold	Saw about ten house martins in the sky.
4th May	Cold, grey	Saw house martin dipping down to muddy path in garden.
6th May	Sunny, windy	Four house martins are building nests all next to each other under the eaves on north side of house.
20th May	Rainy	House martins dart in and out of their nests all day long. Must be feeding their chicks.
10th September	Baking hot	Lots of house martins sitting up on the telegraph wires.
4th October	Overcast	All gone! I hope they find their way back next spring.

Woods and forests

At first, woods and forests can seem dark, silent and empty. But they're actually full of birds, making use of the plentiful food supplies of seeds, nuts, insects and small mammals. It's just that the birds aren't very easy to see. They keep themselves hidden – either from animals who want to eat them, or animals they want to eat. Birds do this with two main types of camouflage.

Jay

Disruptive camouflage– The bird's markings break up its outline, making it hard to spot.

Woodcock

Cryptic camouflage– The bird's colouring helps it to blend in with its surroundings.

The best place to start looking for birds is at the woodland edge, or in clearings. Fewer trees means the birds are easier to spot. Sunny patches in woods also attract insects, and insect-eating birds, such as warblers and flycatchers.

As you go deeper into a wood, keep in mind our top tips for spotting woodland birds. With a bit of cunning and practice, you'll soon be able to make out the birds from the trees.

Nesting sites

The other reason birds like woods and forests is because trees make brilliant nesting sites. Some birds nest in the branches of trees, while others nest in tree trunks. Woodpeckers make their own holes with their strong beaks. When they move out, other birds, such as pygmy owls and nuthatches, move in.

When a nuthatch moves into a nest hole, it plasters mud around the entrance to make it smaller, so other creatures can't get in.

Too-whit, too-whoo

If you're fascinated by owls, then try and go birdwatching in woods at night. It should be called birdhearing, really, as you're much more likely to hear than see an owl.

The first thing you'll probably notice is the call of the tawny owl – *"too-whit, too-whoo!"* This call is actually made by two different owls – a female will call out *"too-whit"* and a male will answer *"too-whoo"*.

HANDY HINTS

County bird reports – available from your local library – will tell you where owls are most likely to be found, and where they roost (sleep) during the day. Keep very quiet if you visit, as owls need their sleep.

A tawny owl landing on its perch. If you can find a recording of tawny owl calls, practice imitating them. If you get it just right, an owl might answer back.

Most broadleaved trees have wide, flat leaves, like these:

Oak

Common beech

Most coniferous trees have needle-like or scaly leaves, like these:

Yew

Norway spruce

Other birds to spot:

Blackbird (see p.41)

Blue tit (see p.38)

Chaffinch (see p.40)

Coal tit (see p.38)

Common buzzard (see p.73)

Great tit (see p. 38)

Green woodpecker (see p.41)

Song thrush (see p.41)

Woodcock (see p.73)

Birds to spot

Here are some pictures to help you identify common woodland birds. It also helps to know which kind of wood you're going to, so you know what kinds of birds to look out for. There are two main kinds of woodland: broadleaf and conifer. Broadleaved woods contain more species than coniferous woods, but you'll spot rare birds in coniferous woods which you won't see anywhere else.

Goldcrest
9cm/3.5"
Smallest European bird. Eats spiders and insects. Listen for its "zee zee" call. Coniferous woodland. All year round.

Chiffchaff
11cm/4"
A tiny warbler. Wags its tail as it flies. Sounds like it's saying its name. All types of woodland. Spring and summer.

Willow warbler
11cm/ 4"
Looks so much like the chiffchaff they are best told apart by their songs. Sings a series of notes running down the scale. Edges of woodland. Spring and summer.

Treecreeper
13cm/5"
Look for a bird with a long, curved beak creeping along the trunks of trees. All types of woodland. All year round.

Nuthatch
14cm/5.5"
Sits upside down on tree trunks and under branches. Broadleaved woodland. All year round.

Long-tailed tit
14cm/5.5"
Look out for its tail, which is bigger than its body. Flies in flocks. All types of woodland. All year round.

Northern & Eastern Europe

Britain & Western Europe

Crossbill
16cm/6"
Thickset finch with sharply forked tail. Coniferous woodland. All year round.

Female

Male

Great spotted woodpecker
23cm/9"
Clings to tree trunks. Look for the red spot on its head. Broadleaved woodland. All year round.

Sparrowhawk
Male: 30cm/12"
Female: 38cm/15"
Swoops silently on smaller birds. Female bigger than male. Woodland edges. All year round.

Male

Female

Jay
32cm/12.5"
Collects and buries acorns in autumn to eat in winter. Listen for its screeching cry. Broadleaved woodland. All year round.

Long-eared owl
34cm/13"
Nocturnal, secretive owl with "ear" tufts which it raises when alarmed. Coniferous woodland. All year round.

Black woodpecker
46cm/18"
Largest European woodpecker. Found in many parts of Europe, but not in Britain. Coniferous woodland. All year round.

Red kite
62cm/24"
Bird of prey with forked tail. Lines its nest with wool and sometimes even clothes stolen from washing lines! Broadleaved woodland. All year round.

HANDY HINTS
The best time to go birdwatching is at high tide (when the water is closest to the shore). At low tide, when the water is furthest from the shore, the birds will be too far away to spot. As the tide comes in, they will move closer to you.

Estuaries

Many birds flock to estuaries – the wide, muddy channels where rivers flow into the sea. The best time to visit is during the autumn and winter, as many birds come to estuaries before flying north for the spring. There's plenty of food on offer, such as shell fish, crabs and worms that live in the mud.

How does it move?

Lots of the birds you'll spot will look quite similar, especially the long-legged waders. So don't worry if you can't tell a dunlin from a knot. Waders like oystercatchers, with their long orange-red beaks, and ringed plovers, which have robbers' masks, are much easier to identify.

You can also tell some birds apart by the way they feed. While oystercatchers pick over the surface of the mud in search of mussels and limpets, dunlins probe deeply, rapidly prodding one muddy spot, then running on to the next.

Dunlin

Oystercatcher

Ringed plover

Dunlin

Knot

Marsh harrier

Bearded tit

Brent goose

Marshes

Marshes are low, wet patches of land in which reeds grow, along with other water-loving plants. There are plenty of birds to spot in marshes all year round, but you'll have to keep very quiet and still to see them. The birds are very secretive and like to hide amongst the reeds. It's best to go on a day which isn't windy, because then you'll be able to spot birds moving in the reedbeds, and hear their songs more clearly.

The easiest birds to spot will be the ones on the edges of the reedbeds and on the tops of the reeds. You might see a bearded tit perching on the reed tops while it sings. Keep looking up too, in case a marsh harrier is flying overhead.

STRANGE SONGS

Some of the birds you'll spot in marshes don't sound like birds at all. If you think you hear a squealing pig, it will probably be a water rail, and if you think you can hear a foghorn, then there's probably a bittern nearby.

Sedge warbler
13cm/5"

Plump bird with cream eyebrows. Fattens itself up in autumn so that it can fly all the way to Africa without stopping. Marshes. Spring and summer.

Birds to spot

These pictures will help you to identify birds commonly found on estuaries and marshes. Watch out for the dramatic change in feathers in many birds from spring to winter. In spring, males have brilliant, eye-catching plumages to attract mates. In the winter, males grow dull feathers, and look much more like female birds.

Reed warbler
13cm/5"

Listen for its tuneless chattering from within a reedbed. Will sometimes perch on reed tops while it sings. Marshes. Spring and summer.

Reed bunting
15cm/6"

Will often perch upright on longish legs on tall stems. Flight jerky and erratic. Marshes. All year round.

Female

Female

Male

Bearded tit
16cm/6"

Look for its very long tail and listen for its loud "ping" call near reed beds. Marshes. All year round.

Female

Male

Dunlin
19cm/7.5"

Common wading bird. Feeds in huge flocks. Listen for its rasping "schreep" call. Estuaries. Autumn and winter.

Winter

Summer

Ringed plover
19cm/7.5"

Runs in stops and starts. Look for the black tip on its orange bill. Estuaries. All year round.

Juvenile

Adult

Adult
Summer

Turnstone
23cm/9"

Turns over stones to look for food. Makes a rattling noise. Estuaries and coasts. All year round.

Summer

Winter

Knot
25cm/10"

Larger than the dunlin. Chestnut and black in the summer, grey and white in the winter. Estuaries. Autumn and winter.

Winter

Redshank
28cm/11"

You might see large flocks of redshanks on estuaries in winter. Legs and base of bill are red. Estuaries and marshes. All year round.

Water rail
28cm/11"

Secretive bird - listen for its pig-like squeal. Red bill and pink eyes. Legs trail as it flies. Marshes. All year round.

Oystercatcher
43cm/17"

Black and white, with a white collar in winter. Makes a loud "kleep" call. Estuaries. All year round.

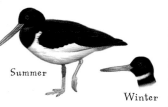
Summer
Winter

Avocet
43cm/17"

Usually seen in flocks. Feeds by sweeping bill sideways through water. Estuaries and marshes. All year round.

Marsh harrier
48-56cm/19-22"

Bird of prey which flies slowly over marshes. Eats small birds and mammals. Marshes. Spring and summer.

Brent goose
58cm/23"

Same size as a mallard. Listen for babbling calls from flock. Estuaries and marshes. Autumn and winter.

Shelduck
61cm/24"

Often in flocks. Looks slow and heavy in flight. Male has red knob on its bill. Estuaries. All year round.

Male
Female

Other birds to spot:

Black-headed gull (see p.63)
Black tern (see p.66)
Common tern (see p.66)
Curlew (see p. 79)
Goldeneye (see p.71)
Golden plover (see p.78)
Lapwing (see p.75)
Wigeon (see p.67)
Woodcock (see p. 73)

Towns and cities

HANDY HINTS

*Look up! Many birds pass through towns when they're migrating.

*Listen out for bird calls. You might hear the "*coo-coooo-coo*" of the collared dove, chattering starlings or screaming swifts in summer.

*Look for birds in parks, in hedges, by rubbish dumps, lakes, reservoirs and canals – anywhere that provides birds with food, water and nesting places.

The black dots against the sky here are starlings, flocking into a city to roost on a winter night.

Lots of birds have adapted to living among people, and make good use of the scraps of food you spill or throw away. You'll often see pigeons pecking at bits of bread in gutters, or picking open rubbish bags to get at the food inside. This extra food comes in particularly handy in winter, when food is scarce elsewhere. Birds that usually live in the countryside sometimes come to cities to feed during the winter.

Birds make use of man-made structures to nest in, too. Sparrows shove feathers and grass into holes in roofs and buildings. Black redstarts used to nest on cliffs, but they've developed a taste for run-down buildings in towns. Jackdaws often build their homes in chimney pots, and kestrels have been known to nest on window sills. Towns are often warmer than the countryside, so some birds come to towns especially to roost at night.

Urban birds to spot

Black redstart
14cm/5.5"

Males black in summer but greyer in winter. Summer visitor but some spend the winter in the south of England.

Female

Male

House sparrow
15cm/6"

Often seen in flocks in city centres, hunting for food scraps. A huge decline in numbers recently. All year round.

Female

Male

Feral pigeon
33cm/13"

A relation of the rock dove. Colours vary from black to mottled to white. Fast and agile in flight. Very common. All year round.

Black-headed gull
37cm/14.5"

A familiar bird. Look for white front edge on wings in flight. Juveniles have duller colouring. All year round.

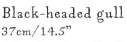

Winter

Carrion crow
47cm/18.5"

Often seen on their own. Call a deep harsh "caw". Thick black beak and black face, unlike the rook. All year round.

Herring gull
56cm/22"

A noisy, common gull. Listen for its loud wailing. Scavenges for food and eats almost anything. Look for red spot on its bill. All year round.

Summer

Canada goose
95cm/37"

A large noisy goose. Look in parks. All year round in Britain. Winters in Denmark and is a summer visitor to parts of northern Europe.

White stork
102cm/40"

Very rare in Britain but common in north-eastern Europe, where it nests on buildings and pylons. Summer.

Other birds to spot:

Collared dove (see p.41)
House martin (see p.39)
Jackdaw (see p.43)
Kestrel (see p.75)
Magpie (see p.41)
Peregrine falcon (see p.79)
Starling (see p.40)
Swallow (see p.39)
Swift (see p.39)

Rivers and streams

When you look at a flowing river or a babbling brook, it's easy to forget how many thousands of creatures there are below the surface. All sorts of birds flock to rivers to feed on the plants, fish, insects and worms that live there.

Some rivers have slow-moving water. These attract swallows, house martins and sand martins, which skim over the river, snatching insects from above the water's surface.

Fast-moving rivers are usually found in high-up places, flowing through rocky, mountainous areas. It's harder to find food when the water keeps rushing by, but the birds that live here have adapted to hunting in these tricky conditions. The dipper can actually walk under water to look for food.

HANDY HINTS

*The best time to go river birdwatching is in the spring and summer, while autumn and winter is the best time to visit ponds and lakes.

*Look for river birds on rocks in the water and in tree branches.

Kingfisher

A swallow catching insects

Grey wagtail

A dipper searching for food

Lakes and ponds

Most of the birds you'll see on lakes and ponds will be ducks, geese and swans. They all have webbed feet, which help them swim, and bills specially adapted to feeding under water.

   Other birds you might see include herons and grebes, which both have dagger-like bills for catching fish, and moorhens and coots, which often come onto land to feed on vegetation.

Dabbling and diving

Ducks can be divided into two groups, depending on the way they feed. There are dabbling ducks, such as mallards, wigeons and shovelers, which look for food just below the surface of the water. Sometimes they upend to reach food further down. Then there are diving ducks, such as goldeneyes, tufted ducks and pochards, which swim all the way to the bottom of the water to catch food.

Shovelers

Dabbling ducks sift tiny plants and animals from near the water's surface.

Shoveler bill

Hair-like teeth inside their bills trap the food, while letting the water flow through.

Goldeneye

Diving ducks swim on the surface but dive under to feed on shrimps, insect larvae and mussels.

WEBBED FEET

Webbed feet act like paddles underwater. The webbing pushes hard against the water, helping the bird swim faster. When the bird draws its foot back, the web closes, so the foot doesn't drag and slow the bird down.

WEBBED TRACKS

Swans and ducks leave webbed tracks like this.

Coots spend time on dry land so they have partially webbed feet.

Moorhens spend most of their time on land, so they have hardly any webbing. They leave much narrower tracks.

Sand martin
12cm/5"

Perches on wires and branches before swooping to catch insects over the water. Digs burrows in river banks to nest in. Rivers. Spring and summer.

Birds to spot

Here are birds to spot on streams, rivers, ponds and lakes. Always go slowly and quietly to the water's edge, so as not to scare birds away. Look up for gulls, terns and insect-eating birds flying overhead. If birds see you first, shy birds such as teal might fly off, while coots and grebes will dive or swim away.

Common sandpiper
20cm/8"

Bobs up and down continuously when feeding and resting. Makes "*tee-wee-wee*" call. Rivers and lakes. All year round.

Black tern
24cm/9"

Black head and body, grey wings. Snatches insects from the surface of the water while flying. Lakes. Spring and summer.

Autumn

Summer

Little grebe
27cm/11"

Diving bird. Makes a whinnying sound, and disappears beneath the water when disturbed. Lakes and rivers. All year round.

Winter

Summer

Moorhen
33cm/13"

Searches for food at the water's edge. Makes a loud "*crorrk*" call. Rivers and lakes. All year round.

Common tern
34cm/13"

Hovers over water before plunging in to catch fish. Rivers and lakes. Spring and summer.

Teal
35cm/14"

Dabbles for food, filtering seeds from the mud. Mostly feeds at night when there are fewer predators. Lakes. All year round.

Female

Male

Coot
38cm/ 15"

Dives for food. Escapes from danger by running across the surface of the water. Look for white bill and forehead. Lakes. All year round.

Tufted duck
43cm/17"

Dives for food. Has a small, drooping crest on the back of its head. Lakes and slow-moving rivers. All year round.

Female   Male

Pochard
46cm/18"

Dives to feed on plants under the water. Look out for large flocks on lakes. Often asleep during the day. Lakes. All year round.

Female
Male

Wigeon
46cm/18"

Dabbling duck. Follows swans and eats plants they have pulled up from deeper water. Lakes. All year round.

Female

Male

Great crested grebe
48cm/19"

They grow their crest feathers in late winter for the breeding season. Growls and barks. Rivers and lakes. All year round.

Summer

Winter

Red-breasted merganser 58cm/23"

Diving duck with a thin red bill for catching fish. Flies fast and low. Rivers and lakes. All year round.

Female

Male

Mallard
58cm/23"

Dabbling duck. In summer, males look very similar to females. Rivers and lakes. All year round.

Female

Male

Goosander
66cm/26"

Diving duck with a long, jagged bill (sawbill) for eating fish. Upland rivers in summer, lakes in winter.

Female

Male

Mute Swan
152cm/60"

Hisses when angry. Reaches for underwater plants with its long, curved neck. Slow-moving rivers and lakes. All year round.

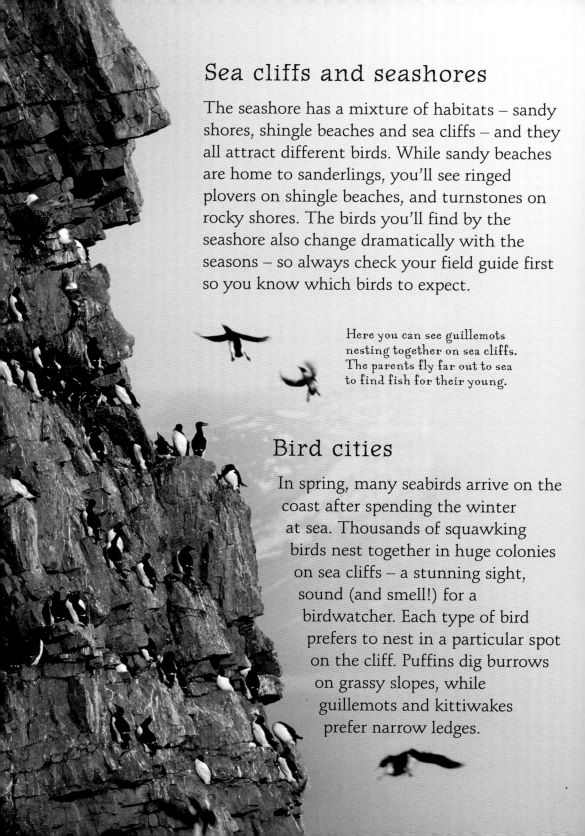

Sea cliffs and seashores

The seashore has a mixture of habitats – sandy shores, shingle beaches and sea cliffs – and they all attract different birds. While sandy beaches are home to sanderlings, you'll see ringed plovers on shingle beaches, and turnstones on rocky shores. The birds you'll find by the seashore also change dramatically with the seasons – so always check your field guide first so you know which birds to expect.

Here you can see guillemots nesting together on sea cliffs. The parents fly far out to sea to find fish for their young.

Bird cities

In spring, many seabirds arrive on the coast after spending the winter at sea. Thousands of squawking birds nest together in huge colonies on sea cliffs – a stunning sight, sound (and smell!) for a birdwatcher. Each type of bird prefers to nest in a particular spot on the cliff. Puffins dig burrows on grassy slopes, while guillemots and kittiwakes prefer narrow ledges.

Living at sea

Some birds spend nearly all their lives on the waves. They survive freezing winters out on the oceans, fly through the fiercest Atlantic storms and dive deep underwater to catch fish. Known as "pelagics", these birds are brilliantly equipped for life at sea.

Diving birds, such as gannets, can torpedo into the sea from 30m (100ft) high, folding their wings just before they hit the water with a smack. Cushions of air under the skin on their head and neck protect them as they dive into the waves.

Some seabirds, such as fulmars, have long thin wings to help them fly huge distances across the oceans. Puffins have much smaller wings. They use them to propel themselves underwater, so they can swim fast enough to catch their fishy prey.

A puffin usually carries between five and ten fish in its bill. The highest recorded number was 61 sandeels.

FISH BILLS

Fish-eating birds all have different types of bill, depending on the size and type of fish that they eat.

Guillemot

Gannet

Razorbill

BIRD ALERT

Some seabirds are in decline because of over-fishing. But fulmars have learnt to benefit from fishing trawlers. They follow them in huge flocks and gobble up the fish waste that the trawlers dump into the sea.

FANTASTIC FACT

Look closely at puffins
and you might notice
their comical displays.
They rub bills, bow to
each other and perform
rolling side-to-side
"funny walks". These
are all different ways
of saying hello to
their mate.

Birds to spot

In summer, look for huge colonies of birds on even the steepest cliff faces, some of which will have come from as far away as Africa and Antarctica to breed on European coasts.

Most of the cliff-nesting birds spend the winter far out at sea, but you'll still be able to see small wading birds, such as sanderlings and knots, which come from the north to feed and wait for the spring.

Sanderling
20cm/8"

Small and energetic, with a straight black bill and black legs. Runs along the water's edge on sandy shores, where it catches tiny animals washed up by the waves. Winter.

Winter

Puffin
30cm/12"

The clown of seabirds, with its colourful bill and bright orange feet. Nests among rocks or in old rabbit burrows. Breeds from April to mid-August.

Rock dove
33cm/13"

Lives on cliffs and in quarries. Listen for its soft cooing. The feral pigeon, which lives in towns and cities, is descended from the rock dove. All year round.

Kittiwake
38cm/15"

A gull with black tipped wings. Listen out as it cries "kitti-waak". Can be seen at breeding grounds from February to August, and offshore during the autumn.

Whimbrel
40cm/16"

Large wading bird with a black stripe on its head and a long bill. Most easily found by listening out for its "pe-pe-pe-pe-pe-pe" call. Spring and autumn.

Razorbill
41cm/16"

Black upper parts and white below, with a thick black bill. Eats fish, especially sandeels and herrings. Breeds from March to July.

Guillemot
42cm/16.5"
Dark brown and white, with a white eye ring. Listen for its loud whirring call. Comes to cliffs to breed at huge colonies from March to August.

Goldeneye
46cm/18"
Look for its white and black wing stripes in flight. Makes a loud "*zeee-zeee*" as part of its display. Visits sheltered bays and estuaries in winter.

Female

Male

Fulmar
47cm/18.5"
Glides close to cliffs on stiff wings. Spends much of the year visiting breeding sites on cliffs, although some spend the winter at sea.

Eider
58cm/23"
One of Europe's fastest flying and heaviest ducks. Usually stays close to the shore. Breeds on cliffs and winters in sheltered rocky coasts and estuaries.

Female

Male

Great black-backed gull
66cm/26"
Very large black-backed gull with a powerful bill. Seen on the coast all year round. Also lives inland during winter.

Shag
78cm/31"
Long necked bird that flies close to the water. Develops a tufted crest on its head during the breeding season. Winters along rocky coasts.

Cormorant
92cm/36"
A supremely skilled fisher. Often seen stretching its wings out to dry them after swimming. Lives on rocky shores all year round.

Gannet
92cm/36"
Large and bright white with black wing tips, long neck and long pointed beak. Best seen in colonies on sea cliffs from January to September.

Other birds to spot:
Black-headed gull (p.63)
Curlew (p.79)
Dunlin (p.60)
Herring gull (p.63)
Knot (p.61)
Oystercatcher (p.61)
Peregrine falcon (p.79)
Redshank (p.61)
Ringed plover (p.60)
Turnstone (p.60)

Heathland

Heaths are good places to spot some unusual birds. Although heathland might look dry and bare, it provides perfect conditions for millions of insects to thrive in. You'll spot insect-eating birds you're less likely to see anywhere else, such as woodlarks, whinchats and hobbies.

One of the best times to visit heathland is at dusk in early summer, when woodcocks and nightjars take to the air to perform their display flights. The woodcock makes soft, croaking calls as it flies, followed by explosive sneezing sounds. Its display flight is known as "roding".

The nightjar usually flies by on ghostly, silent wings, save for the occasional wing clap. Listen for its mechanical churring trill – a sound that can echo eerily around a heath in the gathering dark.

The silhouette of a nightjar on a branch at dusk, in June. When a nightjar perches on a branch like this, it is usually a male *"churring"* to attract females.

Heathland birds to spot

Stonechat
13cm/5"

Call sounds like two stones being knocked together. Nests in gorse bushes on the ground. All year round.

Female

Male

Whinchat
13cm/5"

Look for a small streaked brown bird with white eyebrows. Perches on bushes and fences. "*tic-tic*" call. Spring and summer.

Female

Male

Linnet
13cm/5"

A sociable finch, often seen in large flocks. Linnets used to be kept as pets in cages for their beautiful song. All year round.

Female

Male

Tree pipit
15cm/6"

Nests on the ground. Sings while flying, or from a perch. Call a distinctive "*tee-zee*". Also found in woodland clearings. Spring and summer.

Red-backed shrike
17cm/7"

Preys on large insects and small birds. Stores prey by spiking it on thorns or barbed wire. Spring to autumn.

Female

Male

Nightjar
27cm/11"

Nocturnal bird. Hunts flying insects. Well camouflaged against the ground where it nests during the day. Spring and summer.

Hobby
33cm/13"

Feeds on large flying insects, especially dragonflies, and small birds. Flies with rapid wingbeats and short, fast glides. Spring and summer.

Woodcock
34cm/13"

Nocturnal bird. Hard to spot amongst dead leaves on the ground because of its cryptic camouflage. All year round.

Common buzzard
54cm/21"

Large bird of prey. Feeds on rabbits and other small mammals, and worms. Call sounds like a cat mewing. All year round.

HANDY HINTS

*The best time to visit arable (crop) farms is in winter. Birds find it easiest to look for food in the soil before the crops start to grow.

*In damp grazing land, you might see waders such as oystercatchers searching for worms.

*Look out for barn owls in grazed fields at dusk.

RURAL RULES

*Keep to public footpaths when crossing farmland.

*Shut gates after you, to stop animals escaping.

*Don't touch farm machinery: it can be really dangerous.

Farmland

Everything from corn to cabbages to cattle provides rich pickings for birds. Lapwings, golden plovers and geese flock to crop fields in winter to feed on seeds and worms. Livestock attract plenty of insects, which in turn attract birds such as swallows and yellow wagtails.

But it's the edges of fields that attract the most birds – hedgerows are full of life all year round. There will be plenty of birds nesting in them in spring and early summer.

Also look out for shy partridges crouching on the ground, pheasants dashing out of hedges and sparrowhawks flying overhead.

Under threat

Modern farming methods have changed the countryside, with fewer hedgerows and a much less varied habitat for birds. This, along with the use of chemical sprays to kill insects, has meant that once common farmland birds, such as yellowhammers, skylarks and tree sparrows, are now under threat.

A yellowhammer - an increasingly rare sight. Listen for its song, easily remembered as, "a-little-bit-of-bread-and-no-cheese."

Farmland birds to spot

Tree sparrow
14cm/5.5"
Smaller and shyer than the house sparrow. Often mixes with flocks of finches to feed on grain in stubble fields. All year round.

Skylark
18cm/7"
Sings while over open fields. Has a small crest which it raises when alarmed. Also found on moors and heaths. All year round.

Turtle dove
28cm/11"
Has black and brown turtle-shell pattern on its wings. Listen for its soft purring song in the summer. Spring and summer.

Lapwing
30cm/12"
Looks black and white from a distance, but has a green and purple sheen on its wings. Flocks in winter. All year round.

Grey partridge
30cm/12"
Spends most of its time on the ground, and can be confused for lumps of earth or large stones. Only flies when absolutely necessary. All year round.

Kestrel
34cm/13"
Well known for the way it hovers when hunting, especially alongside motorways. Some nest in towns. Widespread and common. All year round.

Barn owl
34cm/13"
Makes shrieking, hissing and snoring noises. Nests in barns or old trees. Hunts by flying close to the ground. All year round.

Rook
46cm/18"
Forms large nesting groups, called rookeries, in tall trees. Looks like carrion crow but has bare skin at the base of its beak. All year round.

Pheasant
Female 58cm/23"
Male 87/34"
Looks for food on the ground. Runs or flies when disturbed. Roosts in trees. All year round.

Male   Female

Moors and mountains

Wide, empty moors and steep mountain slopes are among the hardest places to go birdwatching. You can walk for hours, often blasted by wind and soaked by rain, without seeing a thing. Despite the vast expanses of land there are very few birds, as there's little food for them to eat. So why bother to look there? Well, because the birds you might see are some of the most exciting of all.

Two young peregrine falcons in a tree in the morning mist. You can tell they're juveniles as they have streaks rather than bars on their fronts.

Birds of prey

Powerful birds of prey hunt for small birds and animals over the moors and mountains. Spectacular golden eagles circle the high peaks, their amazing eyesight enabling them to spot the slightest movement on the ground far below.

Buzzards are about half the size of eagles and tend to hunt on the lower mountain slopes. From far away it can be hard to spot the difference in size, but you can tell a buzzard by its more rounded tail and wings.

If you're really lucky, you might spot a peregrine falcon – a bird famous for its ability to swoop after prey at breakneck speeds. It then delivers a death-blow with its razor-sharp talons.

FANTASTIC FACT

Peregrine falcons can spot prey on the ground from a height of 300m (984ft). When a victim is spotted, the hunter swoops down, reaching speeds of up to 180mph (290kmh).

Insect-eaters

In amongst the heather on the moors and mountain valleys are smaller birds, such as meadow pipits, as well as wheatears and ring ouzels in summer. Meadow pipits flutter up into the air in search of insects, while wheatears keep closer to the ground. They are restless birds that flirt their tails and bob up and down.

Ring ouzels are usually shy and wary. You might see them hurtling recklessly down the cliffs and over boulders in search of cover.

Breeding grounds

Gamebirds, such as grouse, live on the moors and mountains, and are shot for their meat in late summer and autumn. They spend their time crouched and camouflaged in the heather, to avoid predators such as golden eagles. But if you surprise them, they'll rocket up into the air on noisy, whirring wings, calling *"go-back, go-back, go-back"*.

In the spring, other birds come to breed on the moors and mountains. The plump-looking dotterel takes to the mountain tops, while golden plovers nest in the moors and hills.

This picture shows the different birds you can expect to see at different levels of a mountain. The birds are not drawn to scale.

!WARNING!
Be extra careful when walking on moors or mountains. It's easy to get lost and the weather changes quickly. Keep to paths and wear warm clothes.

Golden eagle

Ptarmigan

Snow line

Ring ouzel
Rocky areas

Buzzard

Dotterel

Moorland

Red grouse

Whinchat

Golden plover

Ptarmigans have
feathers on their feet
to keep them warm in
winter. The feathers
also act as snow
shoes, so they can
walk on snow
without sinking in.

Birds to spot

All these birds can be seen on moors or
mountains, although most are found on the
moors and lower mountain slopes, with very
few living on the stark mountain peaks.

The best time to visit is in spring and
summer, when birds which spend the winter
on lowland fields or estuaries, come to the
moorland slopes and boggy mountain valleys
to breed.

Meadow pipit
15cm/6"
Most common moorland
bird. Marks territory in
summer by singing as it
flies up into the air and
then parachutes down.
Upland areas in summer,
lowland areas in winter.

Wheatear
15cm/6"
Nests in burrows,
or among stones -
sometimes in stone walls.
Hovers while looking for
insects to eat. Moorland.
Spring and summer.

Great grey shrike
24cm/9"
Perches on bushes or
trees before swooping and
pouncing on small birds
and voles. Sometimes
hovers. Moorland.
Autumn and winter.

Ring ouzel
24cm/9"
Related to the blackbird.
Sings as it perches on
rocks. Upland moorland
and mountains. Spring
and summer.

Female

Male

Golden plover
28cm/11"
Will chase each other
high in the air in spring.
Upland moorland in
spring and summer,
lowland in winter.

Summer

Winter

Ptarmigan
34cm/13"
Plump gamebird. Grey-
brown in summer, white
in winter. Lives on the
very highest and coldest
moorland and on
mountains. All
year round.

Winter

Autumn

Red grouse
36cm/14"

Found only in Britain. Bursts out of heather when disturbed and flies to safety before gliding back to cover. Upland moorland. All year round.

Willow grouse
36cm/14"

Lives in northern Europe. Not found in Britain. Closely related to the red grouse. Upland moorland and mountains. All year round.

Winter

Summer

Short-eared owl
37cm/14.5"

Hunts over moorland in daytime and at dusk. Nests on the ground. Lowland moorland. All year round.

Peregrine falcon
38-48cm/15-19"

Blue-grey bird of prey with a black moustache. Breeds on moorland, cliffs and mountains. All year round.

Black grouse
Female: 41cm/16"
Male: 53cm/21"

Male has a fleshy red crest over its eye known as wattle. Edges of upland moorland. All year round.

Female

Male

Curlew
48-64cm/19-25"

Nests on moors. Seen on coasts and estuaries at other times of the year. Listen for its loud, ringing "coour-li" song.

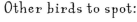

Raven
64cm/25"

Very large black bird which feeds on carrion (dead animals). Nests in high, rocky areas. Mountains. All year round.

Golden eagle
83cm/33"

Huge, solitary bird of prey. Appears dark at a distance, but close-up will show its yellowish golden crown. Moors and mountains. All year round.

Other birds to spot:

Buzzard (p.73)
Carrion crow (p.63)
Dunlin (p.60)
Mistle thrush (p.41)
Nightjar (p.73)
Skylark (p.75)
Stonechat (p.73)
Whimbrel (p.70)
Whinchat (p.73)
Wren (p.40)

Glossary

Here are some words in the book you might not know. Any word in *italics* is defined elsewhere in the glossary.

bill Another word for a bird's beak, often used for water birds.

bird of prey A bird with strong talons and a sharp hooked beak that hunts other animals.

breeding season The time of year when birds build nests, mate, lay eggs and raise young.

camouflage Body markings which help an animal to blend in with its background.

dabbling Looking for food just below the surface of the water.

display A pattern of movement used for communication, especially during courtship and to show aggression.

field guide A bird identification book.

flight feathers The long *primary* and *secondary* wing feathers used for flight.

flight path The pattern a bird makes as it flies.

flock A group of birds feeding or travelling together.

gamebird A bird that is hunted for its meat.

gliding flight A smooth flight in which wings are held stiffly to catch air currents.

habitat A type of place where a group of animals or plants lives.

hovering flight Flying to stay in one place by quickly moving wings in a non-stop figure-of-eight.

juvenile A young bird in full *plumage*. A bird's juvenile plumage is often different from its adult plumage.

migration The movement of some species from one area to another at certain times of year.

moulting The process of shedding and replacing feathers.

nestling A baby bird in a nest that cannot fly.

pellet A compact parcel of undigested food that has been regurgitated.

perch A resting place above ground on which a bird lands or *roosts*.

plumage All of a bird's feathers.

predator An animal that hunts and kills other animals for food.

prey An animal hunted by other animals for food.

primary One of the large outer wing feathers.

reed A tall grass that grows in shallow water.

A pied avocet chick foraging for food on mud flats

roost A place where a bird sleeps.

secondary One of the inner wing feathers.

shaft The central part of a feather.

soaring flight A way of flying that uses up-currents of warm air to gain height.

species A type of plant or animal that breeds with others of its kind and can produce young.

territory An area occupied by a bird or groups of birds.

upending Feeding by tipping upside down, so a bird's head is below the surface of the water and its tail is in the air.

wader One of a group of birds that live close to water and use their long legs for wading in search of food.

webbed feet Feet which have a layer of skin stretched between the toes.

wing bar A natural mark across a group of feathers on a bird's wing.

Trees

Green giants

Trees are some of nature's most amazing creations. When you see a mature tree, you're looking not only at a large plant, but at a living thing that may have existed before your grandparents' grandparents were born, a giant that came from a seed no bigger than your nose.

What makes a tree a tree?

In many ways, a tree is just like any other plant. If you compare, say, an oak tree and a daisy, you can see why. Both of them have roots below the ground and green leaves above (for part of the time, anyway). Both once grew from seeds and they both grow flowers and fruits, too.

So, what does make trees trees? Firstly, they have woody trunks rather than fleshy stems, and they have branches growing from them. Secondly, trees can usually grow much, much bigger than other plants. Although there isn't an official minimum height to qualify, plants aren't usually called trees unless they can grow at least 6m (20ft) tall.

Supported by its thick, woody trunk, an English oak tree can grow up to 23m (75ft) and live for over 200 years.

By comparison, a daisy plant grows to about 10cm (4in) each year then dies back to its roots. Its whole life is over in a few years.

Thirdly, and most impressively, trees can live longer than any animal or any other plant on the planet. You can watch a poppy grow and die in a year, but an oak tree might live beyond its 600th birthday. The oldest known tree in the world is over 4,800 years old, and still growing.

Life-support machines

At first glance, trees may not appear to do much, but they may be very busy: sheltering animals, or feeding them with their fruits and seeds, protecting the soil with their roots, cleaning the air with their leaves... their influence is everywhere. If you sit on a wooden bench to eat an apple and read a book, every one of those things was once part of a tree. In fact, without trees, life as you know it just couldn't exist.

DID YOU KNOW?
Trees first appeared on Earth about 370 million years ago. In time, thick forests grew over nearly all the land but now, trees cover less than one third of it. Over 100,000 different kinds of trees have been identified so far.

Not just a pretty sight, forests like this one provide homes for thousands of birds and other animals.

Western hemlock leaves and cone

There's a clear difference between a typical conifer (above) and a typical broadleaf (below).

Tree types

No matter how different they look, almost all trees belong to one of two groups: broadleaves or conifers. Conifer trees grow cones containing seeds, and their leaves are mostly needle-like or small and scaly. The leaves of broadleaved trees, on the other hand, tend to be wide and flat.

Broadleaves

Many, though not all, broadleaves are deciduous, which means they lose their leaves in autumn. The leaves' flat surfaces help them soak up plenty of sunlight, but water is quickly lost into the air, in the same way as large, shallow puddles dry up more quickly than smaller, deeper ones after a shower.

Broadleaves, like this maple, often turn spectacular colours in autumn.

Tropical trees are broadleaves that only grow in very hot, damp areas such as rainforests and swamps, so you won't see them in Europe. All trees need sunlight and water to grow. Having access to so much of both of these allows tropical trees to grow fast and large, often crowding very close together as they fight for space.

Many tropical trees provide foods, including the cacao pods used to make chocolate.

Cacao tree flowers...

...ripen into cacao pods.

The rainforest contains so many trees, they have to grow in layers. The tallest ones dwarf their neighbours...

...which in turn look down on the lowest level. With so many trees above, the forest floor is often as dark as night.

DID YOU KNOW?

Rainforests cover only 6% of the land on Earth, yet they're home to two-thirds of all its plant and animal species.

Palm trees also prefer hot weather, but need less moisture than tropical trees. If you live in Britain, you'll rarely see palms growing outside, although they can manage well indoors as house plants. You'll know a palm when you see one because its large leaves usually grow in a bunch at the top of the trunk.

No side branches

Many palm trees have bendy trunks, so they don't break in severe tropical storms.

Conifers

The most familiar kinds of conifers are the spiky ones you see at Christmas or in pictures of snowy scenes. There are only about 600 types of conifer, compared with tens of thousands of broadleaves, but they're found almost worldwide, especially in dry or cold areas where broadleaves can't survive.

Conifers can be most easily recognized by their thin, needly leaves or sturdy little scales. Most are evergreens, which shed leaves throughout the year instead of all in one go in autumn. The trees are usually tall and cone- or rocket-shaped, although some develop a round top like a broadleaved tree. Conifers have cones with seeds inside them. The word comes from Latin, meaning "cone carrying".

Even ice and snow are no match for these tough, waxy conifer needles.

Western red cedar

Some conifers have sprays of small, scale-like leaves.

Pine cone

Many types of cones are brown and woody.

Keep an eye out for these two common shapes of conifer trees.

Western hemlock

Shore pine

As they get older, many conifers lose their lower branches.

One of a kind

Some trees are much harder to categorize and don't really belong to conifers or broadleaves. Ginkgo trees, also known as maidenhair trees, are the only living relatives of a type of tree that first appeared on Earth over 250 million years ago. Ginkgoes used to grow only in China, but now you might see them in parks or planted along streets all over the world.

A ginkgo leaf is a distinctive fan shape, and very soft to touch.

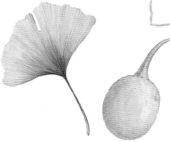

Ginkgo fruits look like small, yellow plums.

The leaves turn a rich yellow in autumn before falling.

Tree or shrub?

Trees that grow in tough conditions, or are deliberately trimmed, sometimes stay quite small. These smaller, bushy trees are often known as shrubs, especially if they have several stems branching from near the ground. Most shrubs are broadleaved, but there are a few shrubs that are conifers, too. Some small, woody plants, such as lavender, are also called shrubs.

Juniper can be a tree or a shrub, depending whether it's more or less than 6m (20ft).

89

Oak buds grow
in lumpy clumps.

Aspen

Rowan

An aspen leaf is one
single piece, while a
rowan leaf has lots
of small leaflets.

Looking for clues

When you're out and about, stop and look at the trees around you. You may be able to tell quite easily whether they're broadleaves or conifers, but you'll need more clues to find out exactly what kind of trees they are. Fortunately, there's always something that'll help you find a tree's identity.

Spring and summer

Spring is the time of year when buds are unfurling into flowers and fresh, young leaves. Early in the season, get in close and examine the buds before they open. Are they sticky, scaly, hairy, or bumpy? This is also the only time you can see a tree's flowers, so take the opportunity to have a good look. Some are like garden flowers, with soft petals and a sweet scent, while others are dull and lumpy, with no particular smell at all.

In the summer's heat, the flowers die off but the leaves keep developing. As well as obvious things like their size and shape, notice how they're arranged on the twig, and whether they grow in ones or groups.

Cherry trees in spring look
almost as if they're made
of nothing but flowers.

Autumn and winter

In autumn, the days get shorter and many trees lose their leaves. Luckily, though, there's something new to spot: fruits and nuts. These come in many shapes and sizes, from bead-like berries and tough nuts to woody cones. Look for them on the ground, being eaten by birds, or even up above, being blown through the air.

Not all fruits can be eaten. These larch cones are fruits, but you wouldn't want to take a bite.

Fruits aren't always soft and fleshy – these tough acorns are oak tree fruits.

A bare tree in winter might look dead, but it's just "sleeping" through the cold weather. Now's the perfect time to stand back and look at the tree's overall shape.

Stripped of its leafy coat, the trunks and branches of this common alder are easy to see.

You can recognize a Scots pine tree by its reddish or pinky-grey upper bark that flakes off in "plates".

Silver birch bark feels smooth to the touch, and has a subtle silvery sheen.

Finally, remember that any season is good for taking a close look at a tree's bark.

Using tree field guides

If you're setting out into the countryside (or town, or park, or garden) hoping to identify each tree you see, it'll help if you can take along a field guide for trees. Most of them separate broadleaves from conifers, then arrange trees in smaller family groups, based on features such as the shape and arrangement of their leaves.

Below, you can see the kind of information you will find in a typical field guide for trees, although it varies from book to book. There's a short guide at the end of this section, starting on page 138.

Most field guides show a leaf and a flower. Some show a picture of the whole tree and a close-up of its bark, too.

HORSE CHESTNUT

Species: *Aesculus hippocastanum*
Family: *Hippocastanaceae*
Habitat: Mountain woods

This is where the tree usually grows wild.

A tree's Latin scientific names may not be the ones you know them by.

Height: 30m (100ft)

This is the maximum height an adult tree would normally reach.

White petals with yellow or, later, pink patches

Prickly fruit with conkers inside

Vital statistics

A good field guide will tell you how tall a tree can grow, so it's useful to know the height of a particular tree you've seen. Forget ladders and enormous tape measures, all you need is a friend and a calculator, or a good head for sums.

If your friend is 1.5m (5ft) tall, and the tree is roughly six times taller, the tree is about 9m (30ft) tall.

Before you start, find out exactly how tall your friend is. Ask him or her to stand next to the tree you want to measure, then walk a little way away and look carefully. Imagine lots of copies of your friend, one above the other. How many of them do you think it would take to reach the top of the tree? You can then multiply this number by your friend's height to estimate the height of the tree.

To measure a very thick trunk, give a friend one end of the tape and walk around the tree with the other until you meet.

To measure the distance around a tree's trunk (its girth, in tree-speak), put a tape measure around the trunk at your chin height. If a tree has several trunks, measure its thickest one.

You could jot down notes about trees and draw sketches of them, so if you see a tree you don't know and haven't got a field guide, you can look it up later.

HANDY HINTS

Useful details to note:
• Where the tree was
• Its height
• Shape of leaves
• Appearance of any buds, flowers or fruit

Life begins

Even the mightiest tree starts life as a
fragile seedling and growing up is slow,
hard work. Here you can read the story of
a young sycamore tree, but you'll find that
most trees grow in a similar way.

From seed to seedling

1. A tree starts to grow in spring from a seed.
With the help of food stored inside it, the seed
sends down a root into the soil to suck up water
and minerals, which it needs so it can grow.

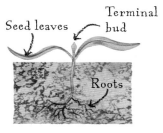

Seed — Root

2. A tiny shoot pushes its way up out of the seed
towards the light. Two fleshy leaves unfurl, with
a bud in between. These seed leaves are usually
shaped differently from the tree's normal ones.
The bud at the tip of a shoot is the terminal bud.

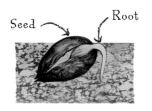

Seed leaves — Terminal bud — Roots

3. The seedling grows, using food stored in the
seed. Soon the bud opens and the real leaves
unfurl. When they're no longer needed, the seed
leaves die. During the summer, a bud forms at
the base of each leaf. The roots get longer,
sprouting smaller side roots, too.

Leaves — Seed leaves

4. In autumn, the leaves change colour and
drop off, leaving a mark called a scar on the
stem. The buds at the end of the shoot are
ready to open up next spring.

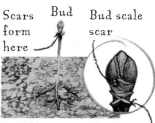

Scars form here — Bud — Bud scale scar — Leaf scar

Getting stronger

In the second spring of the seedling's life, its buds open, making new leaves and a new shoot. Buds on the stem may develop into side shoots. When autumn returns, the leaves drop off. You'll see these same things happening year after year.

Each year, the seedling's stem becomes thicker and taller and develops more side shoots and leaves. Eventually, the stem becomes a trunk, and the side shoots grow into branches. Instead of a fragile plant, it's now a young tree, but there's still lots more growing to do...

This shoot is no longer than a pencil, but many, many years from now it will be a giant sycamore tree.

1. This seedling is in its first growing season.

Terminal bud

Seeds leaves were here

Roots

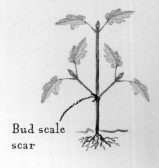

2. This seedling is in its second growing season.

Bud scale scar

3. This seedling is in its third growing season.

Bud scale scar

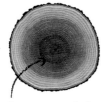

In the centre of the tree is heartwood. This is the oldest part, made mostly of dead water-carrying tubes.

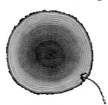

Around the heartwood is the sapwood, which brings water up from the roots as a liquid called sap.

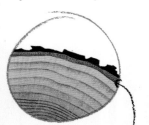

Next to the sapwood is a layer of inner bark, which carries food made in the leaves to the rest of the tree.

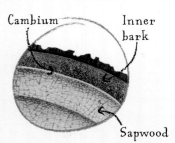

Cambium   Inner bark

Sapwood

Both sapwood and inner bark are made by a thin layer called cambium. It is sandwiched between them.

Inside the trunk

Apart from the growth you can see at the tips of stems and shoots, a tree is busy growing on the inside, too. A very thin layer, so thin you'd hardly see it, makes tubes that carry water up and down the tree. Without these, the tree would die. This layer, called cambium, creates new tubes every spring and summer – so the trunk gets slowly thicker, year by year.

As the tree ages, the tubes harden and die, making the woody rings you can see in a tree stump. There's one for each year of its life.

Peculiar palms

Compared with other trees, palms grow in an unusual way. They have no cambium layer, just clumps of food- and water-carrying tubes around a pithy core. After a palm reaches its adult girth, the only growth is at the top of the trunk.

The inside of a palm is more like the inside of a flower stem than a tree trunk.

Palm trunk

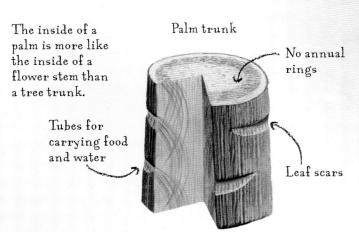

No annual rings

Tubes for carrying food and water

Leaf scars

Growing branches

Branches grow longer each year, but the base of a branch always stays the same height above the ground, no matter how tall the tree is. This is because the trunk and branches only extend at their ends. It would be the same if you only grew at the top of your head and tips of your fingers: your shoulders would always be the same distance from the floor.

Side branches start to grow.

As the tree grows wider and taller, so the branches become wider and longer.

Maples like this need a super-strong trunk to bear the colossal weight of such wide and heavy branches.

A tree that's reached its full height doesn't get any taller, but it does keep getting wider. The girth of a tree trunk usually increases by about 2.5cm (1in) a year. Although this kind of growth isn't as easy to see as the sprouting twigs and buds, it's just as important. Trees are so heavy on top, they need strong, thick trunks to keep them from collapsing under the weight of their own branches and leaves.

Annual rings

Terminal bud

Bud scale scar shows
where the last year's
leading bud grew.

If you cut a twig in two,
the number of rings
inside should match the
number of bud scale
scars on the outside.

This dent shows that
the tree was damaged,
a long time ago.

Annual rings

If you look at a tree stump, you'll
see patterns of rings all the way
across, usually one light and one dark
each year. These patterns are called
annual rings, because the tree makes a
new one every year as its trunk expands.

Counting the number of annual rings in
a tree stump will tell you how old the tree
was when it was cut down. This works
for fallen branches too, as they also have
annual rings inside. Even twigs have them.

Reading rings

The wider one annual ring is, the more the tree
grew in that year, and this is usually linked to
the weather in that growing season. It's
amazing to think that just by looking
at a tree ring, you can tell
whether there was a very
cold year a century ago.

A year with
lots of growth

A year with
little growth

Slow growth years
are usually caused by
wet, chilly weather.

The shape and position of annual rings can reveal more secrets about the history of any tree stump you find. On the right, you can see some examples of ring patterns you might spot.

These rings have a dimple on one side, which means a branch was once growing there.

No two trees have exactly the same shapes and patterns of annual rings.

This tree grew unevenly, maybe because one side was more sheltered than the other, or because the wind bent the tree as it grew.

The first ten years of this tree's life were hard-going, but it started to grow more strongly after that.

You can also look at the light and dark rings. The light layer is early wood, formed in spring when the tree is growing quickly. The dark layer is late wood, made when growth slows down in summer. You can sometimes see these light and dark patterns as stripes in wooden planks, floorboards or fence panels.

Late growth layer

One year

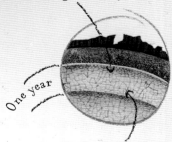

Early growth layer

99

A tree's bark can be as distinctive as its leaves or fruits. Look closely, and feel its surface.

Birch bark peels off in wispy strips.

London plane bark flakes into large scales on older trees.

The bark of beech trees is thin and smooth.

Bark

Bark may seem a bit boring compared with flowers or leaves, but it's one of a tree's most vital parts. You could think of bark as the tree's skin, protecting its insides from damage, just as your skin protects you.

Without bark, the tree's inner parts would be in danger from pests and diseases, or could dry out and die. The bark of some trees, such as giant sequoia, can even help protect them from the intense heat of forest fires.

A thick skin

Bark is made of two layers – the outer bark, which is what you can see, and an inner bark layer underneath that grows every year. The thickness of bark can vary widely from one type of tree to another. Beech trees rely on only 1cm (0.5in) or so of bark for protection, whereas some redwoods are shielded by a generous 30cm (1ft) of the stuff.

A tree's outer bark is dead, so it can't expand as the trunk grows. Young trees have a covering of thin, smooth bark. But, as the tree matures, this splits and cracks and eventually flakes or peels off revealing a new layer. Noticing the colour and texture of a tree's bark can help you look it up in a field guide.

Holey wood

If you spot big holes in a tree's bark, they may well have been made by animals. Bark has natural, small holes of its own, too. These allow the tree to "breathe", taking in air from all around. Air holes are easiest to see on smooth bark, and often look like pale blisters or thin strips.

These rough bands in cherry bark are its "breathing holes".

You can identify a paperbark maple tree by its chocolatey brown bark that peels off in wafer-thin whorls and frills.

Bark rubbing

If you'd like to keep a record of the different types of bark you've seen, you could make a bark rubbing. Here are two different methods to try.

1. This method is the simplest. Place some plain paper on the bark and rub on it with a wax crayon to make an impression of the bark's texture.

2. Put the paper on the bark and rub over it with a plain wax candle. At home, brush over it with poster paint. The bark pattern will remain white.

101

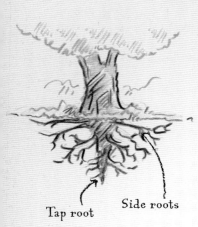

Tap root   Side roots

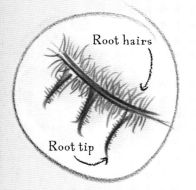

Root hairs

Root tip

Roots

It's easy to forget that a huge part of any tree is hidden away in the earth. Roots anchor the tree firmly in the ground and, most importantly, soak up water and goodness from the soil – sometimes hundreds of litres in a day. They also serve as a food store.

Many trees have a thick, main root, called a tap root, that may grow straight down, deeper than any other. Smaller side roots sprout from it, spreading out to form a tangled mesh just below the soil's surface. These in turn develop rootlets, which are smaller and thinner still. The roots have protective tips that force through the soil as the roots lengthen. Every year, rootlets grow millions of tiny hairs that suck in water and goodness from the soil. This is then drawn up through the roots, into the trunk and to the rest of the tree.

Life in the soil

Armies of creepy crawlies live unseen around a tree's roots. The young larvae of many insects are pests, feeding on the fresh growing rootlets. But there are helpful animals too: earthworms wriggle down from the surface, drawing air and dead leaves into the soil as they burrow. This puts goodness back into the soil, which in turn helps to keep the trees healthy.

DID YOU KNOW?

Banyan trees have roots in the air as well as in the ground. They grow down from the branches and help to prop the tree up.

Size and strength

A tree's roots don't go as deep as you might think. Even the tap roots of most large trees are no deeper than 1.5m (5ft). The really surprising thing is how far out they spread. Like branches, roots can grow longer and thicker each year. Most side roots lie within 1m (3ft) of the soil surface, but they can spread to form a vast web that's even wider than the tree is tall.

Even the strongest roots can't always stand up to a howling gale. Occasionally you might find a tree that's been uprooted in a storm, especially in woods. If you do, it can be an ideal opportunity to get close for a really good look.

If a growing root reaches an obstacle, such as a stone, it just grows around it.

Old roots become tough and woody, creating a wide, stiff "net" to hold the tree in place.

This elm's roots were torn when it fell. Most of them are still left underground.

Two-coloured leaves, like this holly, are called variegated leaves. They're quite rare.

A goat willow's oval leaves are dark green and wrinkly on top, but underneath they're grey-green and rough.

Looking at leaves

There's no better way to start getting to know a tree than by looking at and touching its leaves. The more you notice about a tree's leaves, the easier it will be to look it up in a field guide.

Lift a leaf up, run your finger around its edge, and stroke its surface. How does it feel? New leaves, fresh from the bud, are as soft and smooth as silk, while older ones might be leathery or tough. Some feel crinkly, or sticky, or have sharp prickles or downy hairs.

What does the leaf look like? Is it a broadleaf or a needle, large or small, droopy or firm? What about the length, shape and colour of its stalk?

A leaf can be almost any shade of green, but keep an eye open for subtle or bright reds and yellows, pinks and purples, oranges, greys and browns.

These newly opened beech leaves have baby-soft hairs, which will disappear as they get older.

What are leaves for?

Leaves have the important job of making food to keep the tree alive. Chlorophyll, the chemical that makes leaves green, soaks up sunlight. The leaf then uses energy from the sunlight to combine water with carbon dioxide gas from the air, and turn it into nourishing, sugary sap for the tree. This process also makes oxygen, the gas in the air that you breathe, so leaves are very important for people and animals, too.

If you look closely at a leaf, you'll see a network of veins spreading across it. Water travels up through root, trunk, branch and twig from the soil, then through the veins into the leaves. The veins then take sap back to the tree's food transport system. The liquid-filled veins also keep the leaves firm, just as your skeleton stops your body from being soft and floppy.

A leaf's flat surface acts like a solar panel, absorbing sunlight.

The Sun only shines on the top, so many leaves are pale underneath.

DID YOU KNOW?

You may have seen leaves dancing in the breeze, but they can move on their own, too. Very, very slowly, a leaf turns so it's in the best position to face the Sun.

If you put a plant on a windowsill, you'll notice its leaves start pointing to the light after a few days.

The thickest vein is in the middle. Lots of smaller veins branch off it.

Silver maple leaf

A tough stem attaches the leaf to the twig.

Water from the trunk gets into the veins through the stem.

The veins in conifer needles run straight along the leaf, but they are difficult to see.

Broadleaf shapes

The simplest broadleaf shape is called a simple leaf, and it's just a single piece. Simple leaves can be round or oval, heart-shaped or slim, with edges that are ragged, toothed (jagged) or smooth.

A lime's simple leaves are heart-shaped.

Compound leaves are made up of smaller leafy parts known as leaflets. At first glance, they can look like a cluster of simple leaves, but they're all attached to the twig by the same stalk. Leaflets often grow in pairs, either opposite their partners, or slightly offset, but some sprout from a middle point like fingers on a hand.

Many of the biggest leaves in the world are compound, including giant African raffia palms which, at a monstrous 25m (82ft), can grow to the length of a blue whale.

The edge of a lobed leaf wanders in and out in a wavy shape.

Leaves such as this sweet chestnut have a zigzag edge like a saw.

A horse chestnut is a good example of a hand-shaped leaf.

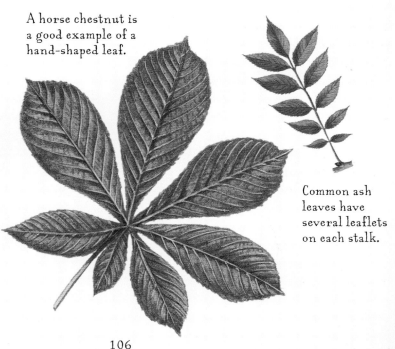

A smooth-edged leaf like this magnolia is called an entire or whole leaf.

Common ash leaves have several leaflets on each stalk.

Cedars have short needles which grow mainly in circular clusters called rosettes.

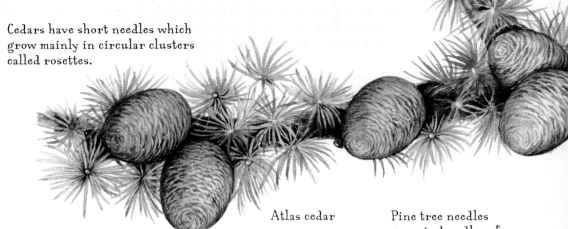

Atlas cedar

Pine tree needles grow in bundles of two, three or five.

Scots pine (twos)

Needles and scales

Almost all conifer leaves are either slim needles or stubby scales, but you'll still find plenty of variety. Just like broadleaves, they grow in different arrangements, shapes and sizes. The world's largest tree, the giant sequoia, has scales that are smaller than your fingernail.

The branches and twigs of monkey puzzle trees are covered with overlapping rows of hard, pointy scales.

Like most cypresses, a Lawson cypress has fine, scale-like leaves.

Monterey pine (threes)

Swiss stone pine (fives)

Sycamore

Maple

Autumn leaves

You'll know deciduous trees are preparing for winter when their leaves start to change. As the autumn days get shorter and colder, the chlorophyll breaks down, and so the green fades, giving way to red, yellow and orange. As well as creating one of the most breathtaking displays in the treespotters' calendar, autumn also gives you a chance to do some activities with fallen leaves you've collected from the ground.

The chemicals that made these rich autumn shades were in the leaves all along, but were hidden by green chlorophyll.

English oak

Horse chestnut

Beech

Rowan

Leaves of northern red oak trees turn reddish brown in autumn.

A leaf scrapbook

A scrapbook filled with pressed autumn leaves can be a decorative and handy reminder of the trees you've seen.

Next to each leaf you could make a note of where and when you found it, and what type of leaf it is.

1. Collect some fallen leaves and wipe off any water or dirt. You'll need sheets of blotting or tissue paper and a stack of heavy books, too.

2. Place each leaf between two pieces of paper and put them in the back of a book. Pile the other books on top and leave for a few weeks.

3. Carefully stick your pressed leaves into a scrapbook with tape, and write all the details you know next to each one.

Leaf skeletons

In fine weather, fallen leaves sometimes dry out and crumble away, leaving behind delicate, lacy skeletons of stems and veins. If you look on the ground in winter, you might find part of a leaf skeleton. You may even find a whole one that's survived. If not, you can create a similar effect by taking a rubbing from a clean, fallen leaf. Put a piece of paper over the top, and rub over the paper with a pencil crayon.

You could keep a colourful record of the leaves you've collected by making a notebook of rubbings.

Tree shapes

You can often identify a tree by looking at its overall shape. To get a good idea of the shape of a tree, it's best to look at it from a slight distance, so you can get the whole tree in view.

Is it tall and slender, or stubby and wide? Do its branches sweep dramatically upwards or droop gracefully down? Or maybe they stick scarecrow-like straight out to the sides?

A tree's shape can help it make the most of the conditions it grows in. Many trees in sunny places have deep crowns – that is, their branches and leaves extend to ground level. They have plenty of leaves to soak up as much sunlight as they can. In woodland, where trees have to compete for space and light, the lower branches tend to die because there is too much shade.

Like this wych elm, many broadleaved trees have rounded crowns.

The branch ends of "weeping" trees bend towards the ground.

Rocket-like shapes are more common among conifers than broadleaved trees.

A Lombardy poplar is one of the few broadleaf trees with a tall, narrow crown.

Dragon trees grow high up in the Canary Islands, where it is warm but often cloudy.

An umbrella-shaped crown soaks up sunlight from above.

The leafy canopy collects water from mist and cloud. It trickles down the branches, into the ground and to the roots.

Trees near the coast often grow bent and twisted, battered by waves or strong sea winds.

Odd shapes

Have you ever noticed that a few trees have weird shapes compared to others of their kind? Lots of things can affect a tree's shape, including the weather, where it's growing, and other trees nearby.

Growing alone, a tree such as this oak is free to spread out.

Closer together, these oaks can only grow upwards, so they're tall and thin.

Trees growing on mountains are often left small and stubby by the cold, dry winds.

A coppiced tree, growing new shoots

Chopping and changing

Sometimes, a tree's shape has been changed on purpose. Cutting a young tree down to a stump, and so allowing it to make lots of healthy new shoots, is called coppicing. Cutting its branches off near the trunk is called pollarding. This is done to control a tree's height. You may see roadside trees that have been pollarded to stop them from growing too big.

Newly pollarded trees often look like twiggy trunks.

Budding growth

A sycamore bud splits open to reveal fresh new leaves, which will slowly unfurl over a day or two.

In winter, many trees seem dead and bare, but if you look closely you can see buds on their twigs and branches. These contain the furled-up beginnings of leaves, flowers and shoots, waiting to burst into life in spring. It's often possible to tell what type a tree is just by looking at its buds, which can be as distinctive as its leaves or crown shape. You could see how many trees you can identify using the bud guide on pages 148-149.

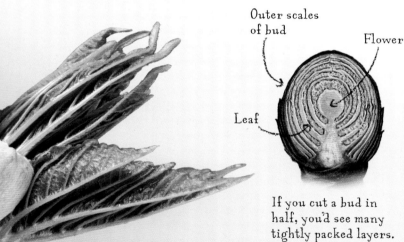

Outer scales of bud

Flower

Leaf

If you cut a bud in half, you'd see many tightly packed layers.

The fine hairs on magnolia buds are as soft as a kitten's fur.

Most buds have thick, overlapping scales to protect the delicate shoot inside from the cold and from greedy insects. In places where there's not much rain in winter, the bud scales also stop the shoot from drying out. Some buds don't have scales at all – instead, their unopened leaves are protected by a thick covering of downy hair.

How buds grow

In spring, when the weather warms up, a new shoot swells and breaks open a bud's protective scales. At the end of the growing season, every shoot will have a new bud at the tip, ready for next year.

Undeveloped twig

Side buds will become shoots.

This horse chestnut twig has sticky, brown buds growing in pairs on opposite sides of the twig.

Horseshoe-shaped leaf scar has a row of black dots.

If this terminal bud is damaged, the bud next to it will become the new leading bud.

Bud scale scar, left behind by last year's leading bud

The main twig is three years old (you can tell by counting its bud scale scars). The side twig is two years old.

You don't have to wait until spring comes to see a bud open up. You could take a twig cutting in early January, put it in water and watch the buds open on your windowsill. Pussy willow, birch, horse chestnut and forsythia are the best trees to do this with.

NEED TO KNOW
Always ask a tree's owner before cutting: and clip the twig – don't snap it off. This avoids the tree being injured unnecessarily.

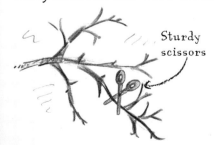

Sturdy scissors

1. Find a healthy adult tree and take your cutting. A 25cm (10in) twig is enough.

2. Put the cutting in a jam jar of water and leave it in a sunny place indoors.

3. Keep the water to the same level. In a few weeks, the buds will start to open.

Ash flowers are tiny purple bobbles. You have to look really closely to spot them.

Magnolias, on the other hand, are hard to miss. They can be big and showy, the size of a fist, with a fresh, sweet fragrance.

Flowers

People often think of flowers and trees as separate sorts of plants, yet all trees make flowers. Without them, they couldn't create seeds to grow into new trees. The way a flower looks and grows depends on the type of tree it's from. Some are big and fancy, and others are so tiny you'd barely know they were flowers at all.

Flowers have male and female parts. Their male bits, called stamens, make powdery pollen, and their female bits, called ovaries, have tiny eggs inside. When pollen reaches the eggs in another flower, the flower is fertilized. It then loses its petals and becomes a fruit with one or more seeds inside.

DID YOU KNOW?

Fig flowers might be the oddest of all tree flowers. They grow inside an unusual pod, which later becomes the tree's fruit.

Fig flowers

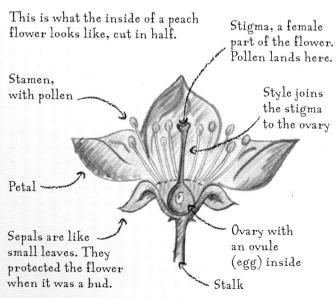

This is what the inside of a peach flower looks like, cut in half.

Stamen, with pollen

Petal

Sepals are like small leaves. They protected the flower when it was a bud.

Stigma, a female part of the flower. Pollen lands here.

Style joins the stigma to the ovary

Ovary with an ovule (egg) inside

Stalk

Flower types

There are three ways that tree flowers grow. Many trees, including conifers, have separate male and female flowers growing on the same tree. Some, such as apples and plums, keep all their male and female bits together in every flower. A few types of trees, such as ash and yew, have their male and female flowers on different trees.

Every one of these apple blossoms has both male and female parts.

It's quite common for trees to have clusters of dangly flowers called catkins. These can be male or female. If you find a tree with catkins and dumpy little flowers at the end of each twig, the catkin is usually male and the other flower is female.

Male flower   Female flower

Holly has male and female flowers on separate trees.

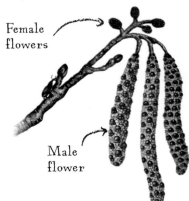

Female flowers

Male flower

Each of the red blobs on these dangling male alder catkins is actually an individual flower.

Style

Stamen

You have to get in close to see a hawthorn flower's stamens and style.

Pollen on the move

Growing flowers is only the first part of making seeds. The next challenge a tree faces is how to spread its pollen from flower to flower. Unless this happens, no fruits can grow.

A passing bee, lured by the scent, lands on the apple blossom.

Pollen carriers

Many flowers "hire" insects to do this vital job. Flowers attract their attention with bright colours or a strong perfume, and many contain a sweet liquid called nectar which insects love to drink.

The point of this isn't to feed the insects, though – it's to bribe them to land, so that pollen sticks to their bodies. Although many trees use bees to move their pollen, there are some trees whose pollen is carried by birds, bats or other furry creatures.

The bee clambers into the flower to drink nectar. Pollen sticks to its body.

An Australian honey possum gets a dusting of pollen as it feeds on nectar in these gum tree flowers.

The bee flies away to another flower, where the pollen rubs off the bee, onto the flower's stigma.

Pretty versus plain

Pollen carriers don't arrive at particular flowers by chance. Many insects have a favourite flower type, usually because of its colour or scent. You can see this for yourself by watching particular tree flowers and noticing what comes to visit.

Butterflies and birds are often attracted to red, pink or purple flowers.

Some trees don't have bright petals, perfume or nectar to offer, so insects tend not to visit them. But they don't need to attract animals, though, as their pollen is spread by the wind. The dangling catkins are covered in pollen, which wafts away as they jiggle in the breeze.

Pollen blows from male crack willow's flowers to the female ones.

Female crack willow flowers

Without pollen carriers you wouldn't find these items on the supermarket shelves.

From bee to you

When pollen from one tree lands on the stigmas of flowers on another one, fruits start to develop. Every year on fruit farms all over the world, millions of bees are brought in hives into orchards, to help spread large quantities of pollen and make sure that plenty of fruit can be produced.

Apples

Almonds

Coffee beans

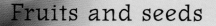

Fruits and seeds

Soon after a flower has been fertilized with pollen, its petals drop off. Inside the ovary the fertilized ovule slowly turns into a seed, while outer layers develop to form a fruit.

Each of these cherries has a stone inside that could eventually become a new cherry tree.

An apple and a prickly conker case are both fruits. But no matter how different fruits look from each other, their job is the same. They protect the seeds they carry and help them get to a place where they can grow into new trees.

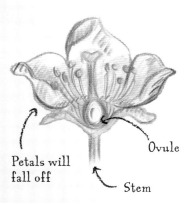

Fertilized peach blossom...

Petals will fall off

Stem

Ovule

The fertilized ovule grows into a seed.

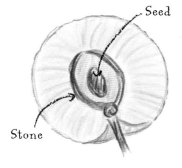

... becomes a ripe, juicy peach.

Seed

Stone

The fleshy layer grows from the stem and the ovary becomes a stone.

Broadleaf fruits

Broadleaf fruits come in a huge range of
shapes and sizes. Many are soft, whole
fruits, such as apples, peaches, cherries
and plums, but they can also take the
form of berries and pods. Some fruits hold
just one big seed, and others have more.

They may look very
different, but all these
fruits come from
broadleaved trees.

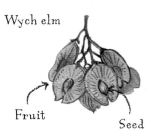

Wych elm

Fruit

Seed

Rowan

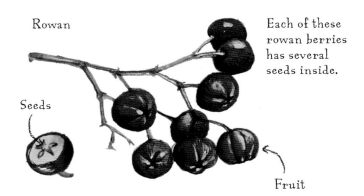

Seeds

Each of these
rowan berries
has several
seeds inside.

Fruit

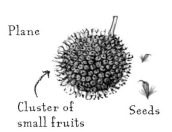

Plane

Cluster of
small fruits

Seeds

Some trees, such as hazels, grow nuts
instead of fruits. But nuts are a type of fruit,
too. It's just that they have a hard outer shell,
which has to rot away or be peeled off or
cracked open to let the seed out. Some have
prickles or spikes to give extra protection.

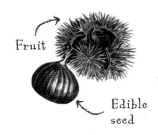

Sweet chestnut

Fruit

Edible
seed

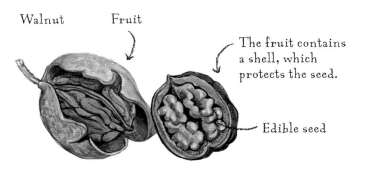

Walnut   Fruit

The fruit contains
a shell, which
protects the seed.

Edible seed

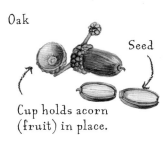

Oak

Seed

Cup holds acorn
(fruit) in place.

Cones

Instead of being soft and tasty like broadleaf fruits, conifer fruits are tough, scaly cones. The scales act like armour, protecting the seeds inside. Cones develop from a tree's female flowers. Once a flower is fertilized, a cone develops and its scales harden and close up.

Over time, the cone gradually turns from green to brown. When it's ripe and ready, it releases its seeds, either by breaking up slowly on the branch, or by letting them drop before tumbling, empty, to the ground.

Some cones stay on the tree for a year, but others take two or more years to ripen. Some hang on the tree long after the seeds have dropped and occasionally cones fall too soon. This is good news for seed-hungry animals – and it also gives you an opportunity to collect fallen cones and take a closer look.

Douglas fir

Male flower

Female flower

1. Cones develop from the female flowers, which look like mini cones.

Young cone in summer

2. When a flower is fertilized, ovules become seeds inside a developing cone. At first, it's green.

Empty cone

3. Most mature cones are brown and hard. The scales open in warm, dry weather.

Pine cones shed their seeds over several years.

Seed

Cone shapes

Cones are more varied than you'd imagine. They can be as small as a pea or as long as your arm; long or round, smooth, knobbly, sticky or crinkly. A few don't even look like cones at all.

Cones can either grow alone or in bunches, like these pine cones.

Young Lawson cypress cones

Cedar of Lebanon cone

Norway spruce cone

Juniper and yew cones look just like berries.

Yew cones

Juniper cones

If it's cold, a cone stays tightly closed.

Hot, dry conditions make it open.

Weather forecasters

People used to say that cones could predict the weather, and there's some truth in that. Cones only open and drop their seeds when conditions are dry. If it starts to get too wet or cold, they close again. If you want to see this happen, just find a closed cone and put it near a hot radiator.

Scattering seeds

It's a tough life for a seed. Many of the fruits that contain them are ruined by insects or disease, or fall off the tree and die before they can ripen. The seeds that are lucky enough to be protected by undamaged and healthy fruits need to get away from the parent tree to find a spot of their own in which to grow. This is so they don't have to compete with the adult tree for water, space and light.

If this squirrel buries the hazelnut to eat later and forgets where it's put it, the nut will have a chance to grow into a tree.

Of course, a seed stuck inside a fruit can't make its way out into the world alone: it needs to hitch a ride. That's why so many fruits, berries and nuts are juicy or delicious. Being eaten is one of the best possible ways to spread seeds.

Tempted by the bright colours of the fruits, birds and other animals eat luscious rowan berries with seeds inside.

The bird flies away. It digests the fruit, but the seed comes out in its droppings, away from the tree, where it can grow into a new tree.

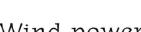

Wind power

Generally, trees that don't need animals to spread their pollen don't rely on them to spread their seeds, either. Their fruits often have fluffy "parachutes" or paper-thin "wings", which catch the wind, allowing them to spiral away through the air like mini helicopters.

Ash (one wing)

Lime (one wing)

Several fruits

If you find any seeds like these on the ground, throw them into the air and watch how they spin down.

With their light, downy "parachutes", willow seeds can easily be carried away by wind or by water.

Sycamore fruits have two seeds and a pair of papery wings.

Willow

Sailing away

As you might expect, trees that grow near seas or rivers, such as coconut palms, use water to carry their seeds. Coconut fruits are hollow, so they float easily, despite their size. Some drift thousands of miles across the ocean before washing up on a shore where they can sprout.

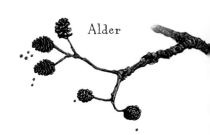

Alder

Look for alder trees near water. Each of their seeds has a natural oily coating, which keeps the seed afloat.

You can have a go at growing any seed you like. If one type of seed doesn't work, just try another.

Sweet chestnut

Apple

Pear

Cherry

Growing a seedling

One easy way to get a really good view of a growing tree is to grow seedlings of your own. You can plant pips and stones from any fresh, uncooked fruit. In autumn, you can try planting nuts and seeds you find outdoors.

Seeds and stones from fruits such as apples, pears and cherries grow well – try growing one of each in separate pots. The amount of time it takes for a seed to grow depends on lots of things, including the time of year and the type of seed. If nothing has grown after six weeks or so, try again with different seeds.

From one little acorn like this, a whole new tree begins.

Grow an acorn

For every seed you plant you'll need:
a flowerpot, small stones, saucer, soil or compost, acorn* or other seed/nut, plastic bag, string or large elastic bands

1. Put a handful of stones in the bottom of the pot, to help the water drain properly. Place a saucer underneath the pot.

2. Add soil or compost until the pot is about two-thirds full. Water the soil until it is moist but not soggy.

3. Lay the acorn on top of the soil. Acorns need plenty of room to grow, so only plant one in each pot.

4. Cover the acorn with a layer of soil. This layer should be about as thick as the acorn itself.

5. Tie the plastic bag over the top. This keeps the acorn moist, so you don't need to water it. Put the pot in a sunny place.

6. After a few weeks, a seedling should appear. When it does, take the bag off and start watering the seedling two or three times a week to keep the soil damp.

7. In the summer, if you can, move your seedling outside in its pot. Carry on watering it regularly. In autumn, you could plant it in the ground.

Water your seedling before you plant it.

8. Dig a hole in the soil a little bigger than the pot. Gently lift the seedling and the soil from the pot. Plant them in the hole and pat down the soil firmly.

*If you're growing an acorn, you need to start in the autumn. Plant an acorn soon after you've collected it, otherwise the seed inside will dry out. You can tell if an acorn is ripe because its cup will have fallen off.

Passing warblers
snatch unsuspecting
caterpillars off leaves,
to feed to their young.

Woodpeckers peck holes
in soft or rotten wood,
and slurp out insects
with their tongues.

A place to live

A large tree is nature's block of flats, with different creatures living and feeding at each level. Birds build nests in the branches. Squirrels and bats set up home in holes in the trunk, while small creatures live in the tree's basement, among its roots. Although all trees attract living things, woods and forests are the best places to see most of the ones shown here.

What's the attraction?

Trees offer food and shelter. There's plenty of space for nesting, and crevices to hide in. Vegetarian animals feast on seeds and berries, while meat-eaters take their pick of the many creepy crawlies that live on the leaves and bark, and even in the wood. Just one big tree can be home to thousands of living things.

Not all creatures you'll find around trees live there all the time – some visit to eat or rest, but live elsewhere. If you watch the comings and goings on a nearby tree, you might be able to work out who's a resident and who isn't.

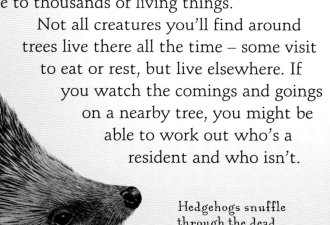

Hedgehogs snuffle
through the dead
leaves at the foot of a
tree, looking for worms
and insects to eat.

In the branches

The branches are mostly used by parent birds for building nests, so their babies are safe from hungry enemies on the ground. Look out for them flying back and forth to the tree with food, or listen for their calls and songs.

Perched on a branch, this robin is singing loudly to announce, "This is where I live - keep away!"

Squirrels sometimes build leafy nests, called dreys, among the branches.

Going down

Many insects live on a tree's trunk and bark, and holes in the trunk can make safe homes for birds and mammals, too. You might also see yellow or green crusty patches on a tree. These plant-like growths are called lichen. They are easily harmed by dirt in the air, such as vehicle exhaust, so the more lichen you find on a tree, the cleaner the air is.

Leafy lichen   Crust lichen

Various lichens grow on the bark of broadleaved trees.

Treecreepers run nimbly up and down tree trunks, hunting insects.

These red underwing moths' wing patterns are good camouflage on bark.

A hole at the foot of a tree might be the entrance to a badger's home, called a sett.

Snails nibble on plants growing under trees.

Life at the base of a tree

Lots of animals rest and hunt for food on the ground at the base of a tree. You're sometimes more likely to see their homes than the animals themselves. Keep an eye out for insects and small creatures such as rabbits, voles and shrews foraging for food.

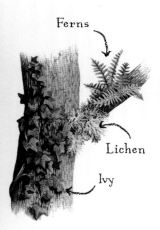

Mouse-sized shrews eat earthworms that they find under fallen leaves.

Ferns

Lichen

Ivy

Primrose

Flowering plants often grow in the shade of the leafy canopy above.

Smaller plants grow on the floors of deciduous woods. The trees protect them, while letting through enough sunlight for them to thrive. Look for ferns, flowers and climbing plants such as ivy, which often grow up the trees themselves. You might also see toadstools and other plant-like growths, called fungi.

Many broadleaved woods are carpeted with bluebells in the spring.

Conifer critters

A coniferous wood can be dark and dense. The tall trees block out much of the light and the ground is often covered with a thick layer of fallen needles. Fewer animals and plants live here than in broadleaved woods, but there's still a lot of wildlife spotting to do. If you're lucky and patient, you may see some more unusual sights, too.

Pine martens live in remote pine woods.

Foxes sometimes raise their cubs in coniferous woods.

Long-eared owls come out at night to hunt.

Spotting woodland wildlife

A good way to explore a wood is to walk slowly and quietly through it, looking around as you go. Animals might run or fly away when they hear you, so it's a good idea to find a convenient spot and sit there silently for a bit. You won't see everything at once, so come back regularly.

HANDY HINTS
Wearing clothes in dull greens or browns will help you blend in better with the scenery. If you have binoculars, you could use them to help you watch birds in the treetops.

When squirrels gnaw cones, they pull off the scales, eat the seeds and leave a rough stem behind.

A blue tit has chipped away this walnut's hard shell to reach the nut inside.

Beechnut eaten by a woodpecker

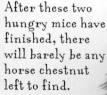

After these two hungry mice have finished, there will barely be any horse chestnut left to find.

Signs of life

You would be extremely lucky to enter a wood and see every animal described in this book, but you can easily hunt for clues to tell you that they've been there. These might include nibbled nutshells or cone scales under a tree, feathers, nuts lodged in bark crevices, shredded cones and even bones and droppings.

Leftovers

Most of an animal's day is spent looking for food, and the leftovers of their meals are obvious signs to spot. Every creature tackles its meal in a different way, cracking, tearing, biting, shredding and gnawing their food to pieces. Look out for teethmarks made by mice and squirrels, or neat, smooth-edged holes pecked out by a bird's beak.

Bark and biting

As well as making holes in bark, animals do other things that leave their mark on trees. Small, furry mammals gnaw bark off or use it to sharpen their claws, while deer rub their antlers on it. Mammals often use jagged bark to scratch an itch, leaving tufts of fur behind.

Bank voles strip bark off trees, to eat the soft layer beneath.

Feathered finds

Droppings and feathers are a real giveaway when it comes to finding trees where birds live, although you might find them anywhere in a wood or garden. Some meat-eating birds also spit out the furry, bony remains of their dinners as small, solid pellets. The best place to look for these is under the big old trees where they like to perch. If you find a pellet, you could try taking it to pieces to see what's inside.

Pheasant body feather

Jay wing feather

1. When you find a pellet, use rubber gloves to pick it up, then put it in a bag and take it home.

2. Using tweezers, carefully pick it apart and lay out the contents on a sheet of plain paper to look at.

A barn owl pellet and its contents

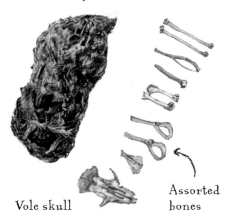

Vole skull

Assorted bones

Wood pigeon wing feather

All three feathers above belong to birds that you might find in woodlands.

Tree pests

Many living things feed on a tree's fruits and nectar, but to some creatures, a tree's sap, leaves and other vital parts offer a more tempting meal. This isn't always a problem. If a tree's leaves are nibbled by insects, it can grow new ones. But some kinds of pests can do more serious damage.

The shape, colour and size of an insect gall depends on the tree and the insect that formed it.

Oak marble gall

Young gall wasp climbing out of hole in gall

Prickly "pineapple" gall

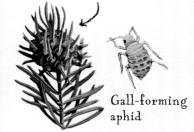

Gall-forming aphid

Cosy eggs

Many insects lay their eggs on trees because they provide a ready source of food when the young larvae hatch. While they are laying their eggs, for example on a leaf or shoot, some types of insect inject it with a chemical. This causes the tree to grow a lump called a gall around the eggs, to protect itself.

Galls also provide shelter and often food, for the larvae. When they are ready, the insects eat their way out. On some galls, you can see an escape hole.

This hazelnut has a side cut away to show a weevil larva growing inside.

Adult nut weevil

Larva

The different types of galls on this oak leaf were caused by different insects.

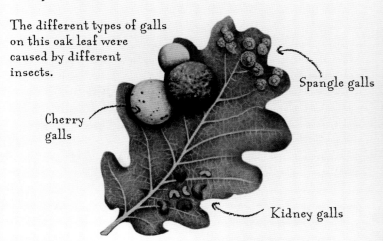

Spangle galls

Cherry galls

Kidney galls

Hungry babies

When insect eggs hatch, the larvae are very hungry. Squiggly marks and holes chewed out of a leaf are signs that it's been hijacked as an insect's dinner. Look out for butterfly and moth caterpillars feeding on trees. Each species mostly lives on one type of tree. So if you look at lots of trees in early summer, you may be able to figure out what eats what.

Some caterpillars, like these sawfly larvae, are a serious problem to trees. Hordes of them can strip a tree bare of its leaves.

These squiggles look like drizzles of paint, but they're not. They're leaf mines, made by burrowing insects eating the leaves from the inside.

This lone moth caterpillar can destroy hundreds of healthy leaves.

Elm bark beetles tunnel under the bark of elm trees, spreading Dutch elm disease from tree to tree as they go.

Adult insects can be as much of a nuisance to a tree as their young, since they tend to be just as greedy. A few carry diseases, too. Dutch elm disease is caused by a fungus, but it is spread from one tree to another by elm bark beetles.

Tunnels

Elm bark beetle

Parasites

Parasites are plants or animals that attach themselves to other living things and suck out their juices, a bit like vampires in horror stories. Parasites usually damage the trees they're feeding from (their hosts), but they hardly ever kill them. After all, the hosts are what keeps them alive.

Mistletoe often grows on apple trees. It makes some food in its leaves, but relies on its host for water and goodness from the soil.

Fungus

Fungus (plural: fungi) is one of the most serious parasites that can attack a tree. Fungi have no leaves so they can't make their own food. Instead, they invade the heartwood in the middle of a tree trunk with thousands of tiny threads. Toadstools (which look like mushrooms) are one type of fungus. There are others that look like enormous plates, lumps of raw meat or blobs of jelly.

These toadstools are clustered at the base of a fungus-infected tree.

How fungus can kill

If a tree suffers serious damage, such as losing a branch or being struck by lightning, that's when fungus makes its move. Tiny spores (like plant seeds) enter the wound and spread through the trunk, rotting its insides and weakening it or causing the tree to die back. It doesn't matter to fungus whether it kills its host or not, because it grows on dead things as well as living ones.

White pine blister rust is a fungus which causes swellings on pine trunks and branches.

Bracket fungus causes a disease called conifer heart rot. It weakens the inside of the tree, which usually later snaps in the wind.

Dryad's saddle bracket fungus

Cuts and grazes

Trees aren't completely helpless against injury, though. Like your body, a tree can help itself if it's only damaged a little. Look on tree trunks for round, smooth spots. These are sealed-up wounds left behind where a branch has broken off and new wood has grown over.

Recent damage

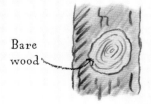

Bare wood

1. When the branch has just broken off, you can see a patch of bare wood, where the branch was. Fungi can easily get in.

Three years later

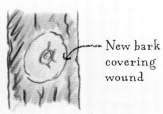

New bark covering wound

2. A new bark layer starts to grow in from the edges. This will gradually grow across and cover the damage.

About six years later

New bark

3. A wound on a tree heals very slowly. In an old tree, the bare wood may never be totally covered.

Life in dead trees

With a bit of luck and the right conditions, trees can live for hundreds or, in the odd case, even thousands of years. All through its life a tree sheds branches, leaves and bark. One day, it will die completely. But other plants and animals carry on living in its remains.

Recycling

When a tree dies, fungi and other creatures too tiny to see, get inside and start to break it down. This is called decay, or rotting. Decay is really important in nature because it releases all the raw materials the tree was made from, and puts them back into the soil. These can then be used by new young plants to make them strong.

Crumbling bark and hollow trunks also carry on providing homes for all sorts of creatures. A third of all living things in a wood rely in some way on dead trees to stay alive.

Even though this tree has died, it's still full of life. It has become home to a mass of moss, fungi and hidden insects.

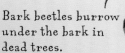

Bark beetles burrow under the bark in dead trees.

Leaf litter and wood piles

When deciduous trees shed their leaves in autumn, the dead leaves pile up at the foot of the tree. These piles, known as leaf litter, form a dark and secret world of damp crevices, a haven for creepy-crawlies and other small animals. Lift up some leaves and see what might be lurking underneath. (But put them back afterwards.)

You don't need to visit a wood to see the sorts of animals that hang around tree remains. Arranging a small pile of dead branches or leaves in a shady corner of a garden will encourage animals to visit and plants to grow. Leave the pile undisturbed after you've made it, then watch what moves in.

Stag beetles live in rotting wood.

Grey slugs munch on fresh and rotting leaves.

Dead leaves are a feast for a passing millipede.

All the animals on this page are attracted to moist, shady wood and leaf piles.

Woodlice scuttle around under rotting bark.

Common toad

A rich mix of leaves and fallen berries like this could feed and shelter dozens of tiny creatures.

Trees to spot

In this section of the book, you'll find pictures and descriptions of common trees and winter buds to spot. Each one has facts you might need to know about the tree's mature height, its fruits and flowers, its bark, and where to look for it.

You can find links to more field guides on the Usborne Quicklinks Website at *www.usborne-quicklinks.com*

Monkey puzzle (Chile pine)

Up to 26m (85ft). Overlapping, glossy leaves covering the shoots. Bristly, ball-shaped cone. Gardens and parks.

Conifers

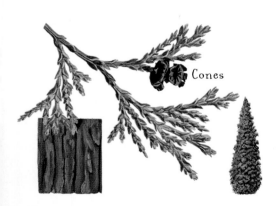

Cones

Lawson cypress

Up to 38m (125ft). Narrow shape. Small, round cones and sprays of scaly leaves. Purple-brown, flaky bark. Often planted as a hedge.

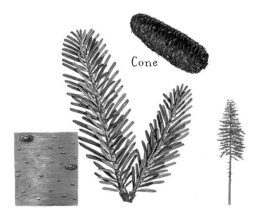

Cone

European silver fir

Up to 48m (157ft). Large, upright cones at top of tree. Flat needles have silver underside. Flat, round scars left on twigs when needles drop. Woods.

Berry-like cone

Yew

Up to 20m (66ft). Male and female flowers usually on separate trees. Smooth, flaking bark. Young cones are green. Woods, churchyards.

Young cone

Adult cone

Western hemlock

Up to 48m (157ft). Drooping branches and top shoots. Reddish flowers and small, brown cones. Needles various lengths. Woods.

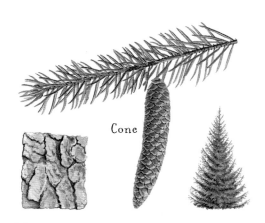

Cone

Norway spruce

Up to 45m (148ft). Long, hanging cones and sharp, rigid needles. Reddish flowers. Commonly used as Christmas trees. Parks, gardens, woods.

Cone

Sitka spruce

Up to 47m (154ft). Long, hanging cones. Very prickly needles. Fat, yellow buds on yellow twigs. Bark flakes off in "plates". Parks, coasts, woods.

Juniper

Up to 6m (20ft). Sharp needles arranged in threes. Berry-like cones turn purplish in second year. Often grows as a shrub. Open spaces.

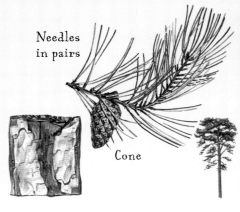

Scots pine

Up to 35m (115ft). Small, pointed buds. Bark is red near top of tree, becoming grey below, peels in odd shapes. Mountains and sandy soil.

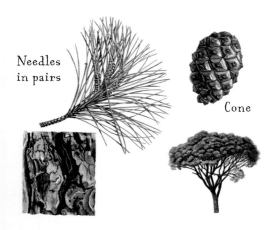

Stone pine

Up to 22m (72ft). Long, stiff, paired needles. Small buds. Green cones turn brown with age. Deeply ridged bark. Mediterranean coast.

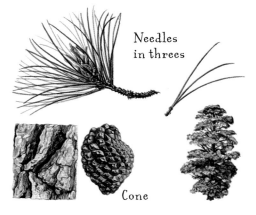

Monterey pine

Up to 30m (98ft). Slender, grass-green needles growing in threes. Dumpy cones stay on tree for many years. Near the coast.

Atlas cedar

Up to 40m (131ft). Large, spreading tree with barrel-shaped cones. Blue-green or dark green needles grow singly or in rosettes. Woods and parks.

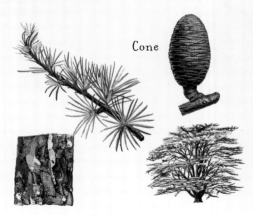

Cedar of Lebanon

Up to 40m (131ft). Leaves can grow singly or in dense clusters. Yellow flowers. Cones like Atlas cedar, but without flattened top. Parks.

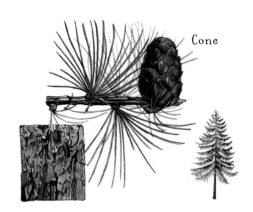

European larch

Up to 45m (148ft). Rosettes of soft needles turn yellow then fall off in winter. Drooping yellow male flowers, red female flowers. Widespread.

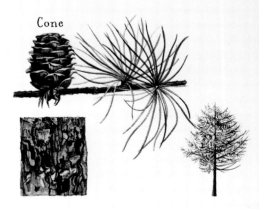

Japanese larch

Up to 37m (121ft). Cones have unusual folded edges. Dark orange-red twigs and pinkish flowers. Blue-green needles fall off in winter. Widespread.

Broadleaves

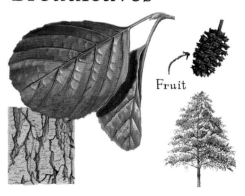

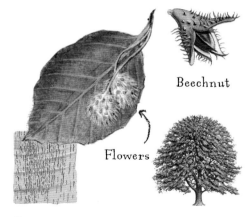

Common alder

Up to 25m (82ft). Catkins in early spring. Cone-like fruits which stay on in winter. Greyish-black, scaly bark. Near water and damp woods.

Common beech

Up to 36m (118ft). Smooth, grey bark. Young leaves light green, but become darker. Fruit has woody husk split into four. Widespread.

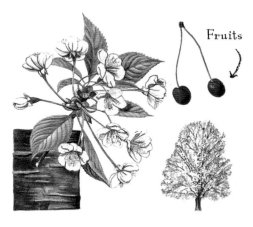

Crab apple

Up to 10m (33ft). Five-petalled blossoms appear in May-June. Smallish yellow fruits edible, but sour. Wild in hedges and thickets.

Wild cherry (gean)

Up to 20m (66ft). Reddish-brown bark peels in ribbons. Large white flower clusters appear in spring. Woods and thickets.

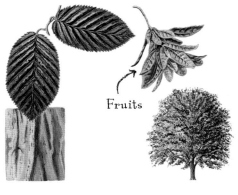

Fruits

Japanese cherry

Up to 20m (66ft). Pink blossoms
appear April-May. Purple-brown
or greyish bark. Many varieties.
Gardens and along streets.

Hornbeam

Up to 20m (66ft). Green, winged
fruits hanging in clusters. Brown
(male) and green (female) catkins.
Smooth, grey bark. Hedges, streets.

Fruits

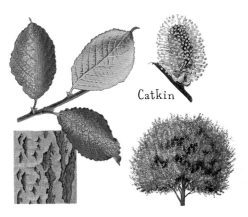

Catkin

Whitebeam

Up to 25m (82ft). Leaves white and
fuzzy underneath. Grey bark cracks
with age. Five-petalled flowers in
May-June. Sour berries. Grows wild.

Goat or pussy willow

Up to 10m (33ft). Silvery-grey
upright catkins in late winter.
Separate male and female trees.
Hedges and damp woods.

Common lime

Up to 40m (131ft). Scented yellow flowers attract bees in June. Young bark smooth and grey, ridged when older. Parks and gardens.

Silver birch

Up to 30m (98ft). Pale bark peels in ribbons. "Lamb's tail" catkins in April. Wild on heaths and mountains, also planted in gardens.

Crack willow

Up to 15m (49ft). Often has more than one trunk. Bluish-grey bark, heavily cracked. Leaves are green on top, silver underneath. Near water.

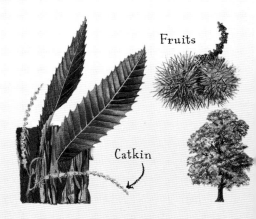

Sweet chestnut

Up to 35m (115ft). Young bark grey and smooth. Often spiral patterns on trunk. Small yellow flowers on long catkins. Nuts in very prickly green case

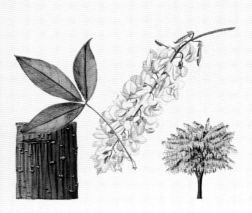

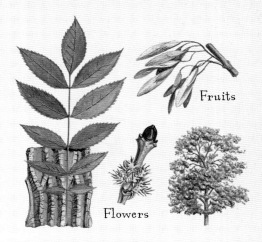

Laburnum

Up to 7m (23ft). Yellow flowers
in May-June. Greenish-brown bark
becomes less smooth with age.
Poisonous seeds. Gardens.

Common ash

Up to 45m (148ft). Grey-brown,
smooth bark, becomes furrowed
with age. Clusters of seeds stay on in
winter. Common in woods and parks.

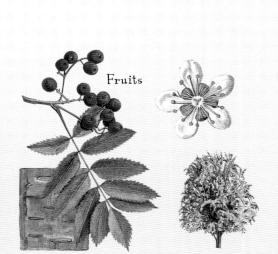

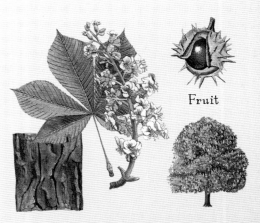

Rowan (mountain ash)

Up to 20m (66ft). White flowers
in May, followed by red berries in
September. Smooth, shiny grey bark.
Wild on mountains.

Horse chestnut

Up to 38m (125ft). Horseshoe-shaped
scars left on twigs by fallen leaves.
Flowers in May. Prickly fruits with
conkers inside. Woods and parks.

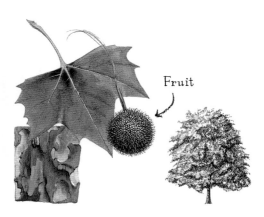

Fruit

London plane

Up to 45m (148ft). Flaky bark which leaves behind white patches. Flowers have no petals. Spiky, round fruits stay on in winter. City streets.

Lower leaves are less lobed.

White poplar

Up to 26m (85ft). Leaves covered with white down underneath. Whitish-grey bark with diamond-shaped marks. Wet areas, open and waste land.

Fruits

Field maple

Up to 26m (85ft). Tiny green flowers in clusters. Narrow-ridged grey bark. Leaves turn golden in autumn. Hedges and woods.

Fruits

Norway maple

Up to 27m (89ft). Dome-shaped crown. Forms yellow-green flowers in spring. Colourful autumn leaves. Parks, streets and gardens.

Sycamore

Up to 35m (115ft). Smooth bark flakes off in large, flat pieces. Winged fruits, called keys, in pairs. Green flowers. Parks and streets.

Hawthorn

Up to 10m (33ft). Thorny twigs. Pinkish-brown bark cracks in oblongs. Small, white flowers in May, berries in autumn. Widespread. Hedges.

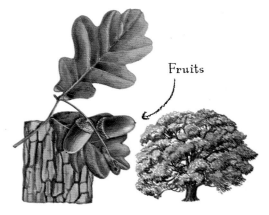

Sessile oak

Up to 21m (69ft). Dark green, long-stalked leaves. Acorns often stalkless. Grey-brown bark with knobbly ridges. Woods and parks.

English oak

Up to 37m (121ft). Wide-spreading branches. Yellow dangly male catkins. Tiny female flowers on end of new shoots. Common alone and in woods.

Winter twig guide

In winter, when many trees have no leaves or flowers,
you can often use twigs and buds to identify a tree.
Here are some easy questions you could ask yourself:

- What colour are the buds and the twig?
- What shape is the twig?
- Are the buds pointed or rounded?
- How are the buds arranged on the twig?
- Are the buds covered in hair, or scales?
- Are they sticky?
- What shape are the leaf scars?

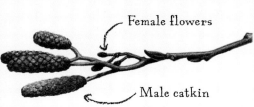

Female flowers

Male catkin

False acacia

Grey twig. Thorns next to tiny,
alternate buds.

Common alder

Alternate, stalked, purple buds,
often with male catkins.

Ash

Smooth, grey twig. Large, black
opposite buds. Leaf scars have a
smile-shaped row of dots.

Beech

Slender twig. Alternate, spiky,
brown buds sticking out.

Wild cherry

Large, glossy, red buds grouped
at tip and along twig.

Sweet chestnut

Knobbly twig. Large, reddish,
alternate buds.

English elm

Zigzag twig. Alternate, blackish-red buds.

Turkey oak

Clusters of alternate buds with twisted whiskers.

Magnolia

Huge, furry, green-grey buds.

Common lime

Zigzag twig. Alternate, reddish buds with two scales.

White poplar

Twig and alternate buds covered with white down.

London plane

Alternate, cone-shaped buds. Leaf scars surround the buds.

Willow

Slender twig. Alternate buds close to twig.

Sycamore

Large, green, opposite buds with dark-edged scales. Pale leaf scars.

Whitebeam

Downy, green, alternate buds.

Walnut

Thick, hollow twig. Heart-shaped leaf scars. Black, velvety alternate buds.

The pictures below show the different cuts of wood that come from this log.

Working with wood

Ever since the first caveman ate a fruit or rubbed sticks together to make fire, people have used trees for all sorts of things: to make boats, houses, furniture, tools, ornaments, medicines, foods and paper. For some people, trees are an important part of religion, too.

Wide planks come from the sides, or all the wood is mashed up to make paper.

From tree to timber

Before a tree can be made into anything, it has to be cut down. Years ago, this was a back-breaking job done with an axe, but modern machines make light work of it. The branches are sliced off the felled tree, then the trunk is cut into logs and taken to a sawmill. A log can be sawn into planks of many sizes, or made into wood chips or pulp.

Heartwood makes strong timber for building.

Wood is full of moisture, so freshly cut planks need drying out, or seasoning, before they can be used. This is done by piling them like a stack of waffles and leaving them in the open air, or drying them in a type of oven called a kiln.

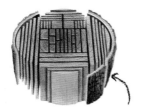

The bark is mashed into wood chips.

Stacking planks with gaps between allows the air to flow around them.

Patterns and marks

When a plank is cut from a log, the annual rings make a pattern of wavy or straight lines called the grain. Wood cut along the grain is stronger than wood cut across it. Round or eye-shaped marks called knots in the wood show where a branch joined the trunk.

You can count the rings in a knot to see how old the branch that made it was.

Knot

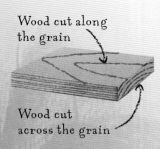

Wood cut along the grain

Wood cut across the grain

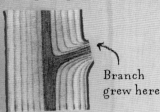

Section of trunk cut along the grain

Branch grew here

The picture above shows the type of trunk that would have created the knot on the left.

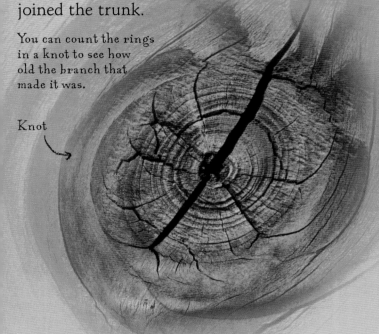

Hardwood and softwood

The wood that comes from broadleaves and conifers is as different as the trees themselves. Conifer wood, called softwood, is used more than hardwood from broadleaved trees, because it grows in more regular shapes and it's easier to cut. Even so, there are many trees of both types that have especially useful wood.

DID YOU KNOW?

Wood isn't the only useful thing that comes from trees. A chemical in willow bark was the source of aspirin. Certain buds are dried and used as cooking spices. Even amber and rubber are tree products – made from sap.

151

A world without trees

These woodland butterflies were once common in Britain, but are now endangered or extinct.

High brown fritillary (endangered)

Swallowtails (endangered)

Trees do so many important things that a world without them would probably be a world without animals or people, either – a sick, filthy, parched wasteland.

Every year, all over the world, vast areas of trees are destroyed accidentally by fires, deliberately cut down for timber, or cleared to make space for farming. When this happens, many animals lose their homes and many die. The ones that survive might move to new areas, but then they have to compete for food with the animals that already live there. So life just gets harder and harder. The unluckiest animals just can't survive the change, and may eventually die out altogether.

Large blue (extinct)

Large tortoiseshell (extinct)

DID YOU KNOW?
Experts think that up to 50,000 rainforest plant and animal species die out every year, as their homes are torn down or burned. The last time living things died out so fast was when dinosaurs existed.

Water crisis

With fewer trees, water supplies start to become dank and muddy. During storms, trees' roots normally help to control the speed at which rainwater flows into streams. But, without them, floods soon wash the top layer of soil away into rivers and streams, suffocating the fish and making the water too dirty to drink.

Choking and frying

As trees continue to disappear, so does the oxygen, which the leaves produced. The leaves also filtered out smoke, dust and ash from vehicles and factories, keeping the air clear and clean. When the trees are gone, the thin, stale air will slowly fill up with dirt and grime.

Trees use carbon dioxide gas from the air. Heat that came from the Sun can escape to keep Earth's temperature just right for living things.

And, if that wasn't bad enough, the world will probably get hotter, too. When plants make food, they use carbon dioxide gas from the air. The remaining carbon dioxide helps to trap heat from the Sun, keeping the Earth comfortably warm enough for life to exist. But without trees to help keep this balance, too much carbon dioxide might build up in the air, allowing less and less heat to escape. This would make the whole planet heat up like an oven.

But the story doesn't have to end like this...

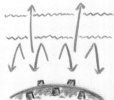

When trees are cut down, more carbon dioxide stays in the air. It traps more heat, warming the Earth like a greenhouse on a hot day.

→ Heat

〜 Carbon dioxide

With modern technology, people can cut down trees quicker than ever.

Making a difference

Everyone can do their bit to protect trees and make sure they live to continue doing good things in the future. The easiest way to do this is to treat them with respect. When it comes to nature, "Look but don't touch" is a good thing to remember.

If you find a tree that interests you, don't pull bits off – the tree needs them more than you do. Just looking at a tree will usually tell you quite a lot about it. For an even closer view, try hunting for pieces it has shed on the ground.

Make sure your family and friends know about the dangers of lighting campfires and barbecues, or smoking cigarettes, near woods or dry grasses and shrubs. Wood fires are very hard to control. With a little help from the wind, they can turn acres of trees into a desert of smouldering ashes in a few hours.

Leaves, fruits and seeds often fall off a tree, giving you an ideal opportunity to have a really close look.

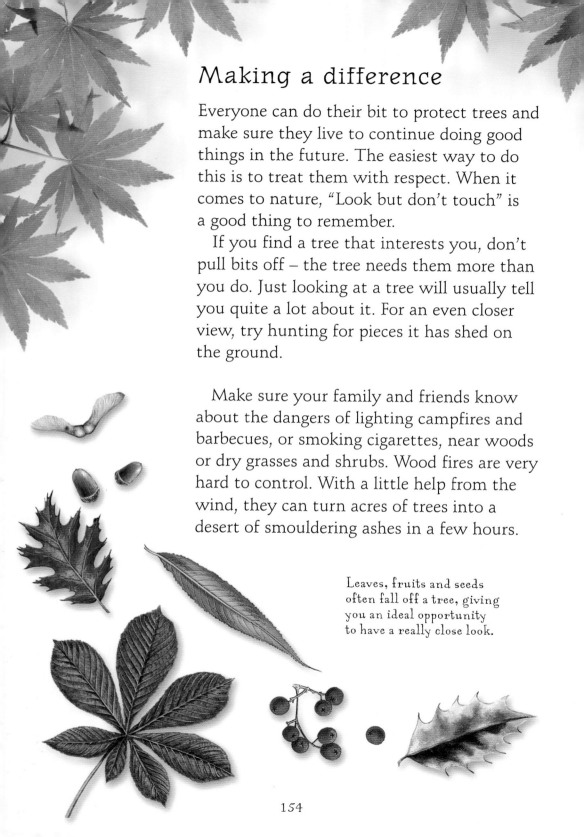

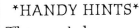

Going further

From time to time there are stories in the news about people who sit in trees to make sure they don't get cut down, but there are other, simpler ways to help protect and preserve trees.

Re-using and recycling paper in your home, and encouraging recycling at school or work, helps reduce the number of trees that need to be cut down to make new things. Try to use products labelled "sustainable" (like this book). This means that for every tree cut down to make it, new ones are planted to replace it.

Another great way to help the natural world, if you want to go a step further, is by planting a tree yourself. You might not have a garden big enough to do this, but there are lots of organizations you can join which are involved with tree planting. There are even companies that will plant a tree in a wood for you, as a gift to another person.

If enough people did something to help, however small, it could make a big difference both for the future of trees, and for the future of the planet.

HANDY HINTS

This symbol on cardboard means it can be recycled.

The more people get involved in tree-planting schemes, the more likely fragile pine saplings like these are to grow into huge, dense forests.

155

Glossary

Here are some words in the book you might not know. Any word in *italics* is defined elsewhere in the glossary.

annual ring A ring of dark and light wood in the cross-section of a *trunk* or branch that shows one year's growth.

bark A tough outer layer that protects the tree's insides.

blossom *Flowers.*

bract A leaf-like part of a cone supporting the *seed*.

broadleaved tree (broadleaf) A tree that has wide, flat leaves. Most are *deciduous*.

bud An undeveloped *shoot*, leaf or *flower*.

bud scale scar A ring-shaped mark around a twig, left when the *terminal bud scales (2)* fall off.

cambium A thin layer that produces new *inner bark* and *sapwood* in a tree *trunk*

catkin An often sausage-shaped cluster of tiny *flowers*, all of the same sex, growing on one stalk.

chlorophyll A green chemical found in leaves that absorbs sunlight to help make food for the plant.

compound leaf A type of leaf made up of smaller *leaflets*.

cones The *fruits* of *conifers*.

conifer A tree with needle-like or scaly leaves, which bear *cones* with their seeds inside. Most are *evergreen*.

crown A tree's branches, twigs and leaves.

cutting A part of a tree, such as a *shoot* or *root*, cut off and used to grow a new tree.

deciduous Losing its leaves over a few weeks, usually in autumn.

entire leaf A leaf that has a smooth edge.

evergreen Losing its leaves throughout the year, so the tree is always green.

fertilization The joining of an *ovule* with *pollen* to make a *seed*.

flowers The parts of a tree where new *seeds* are made.

fruits The parts of a tree that hold its *seeds*.

heartwood Old wood at the core of the *trunk* that has grown too solid to carry water.

inner bark A layer beneath the outer layer of *bark* that grows every year.

leaflets Leaf-like sections that make up a *compound leaf*.

leaf scar Mark left on a twig where a leaf has fallen off.

leaf skeleton The dried-up remainder of a leaf.

lobed leaf A type of leaf or *leaflet*, partly divided into sections called lobes.

nectar A sweet, sticky liquid produced by *flowers* to attract insects.

ovary A female part of a *flower* that contains *ovules*.

ovule A plant "egg".

pollen A powder made by the *flower's* male parts for transfer to the female parts to make *seeds*.

rootlet The smallest of *roots*.

roots Parts of a tree that grow into the ground, absorbing water and goodness from the soil and anchoring the tree.

sap A liquid that carries sugars (food made in the leaves) around the tree.

sapwood The outer area of wood in a tree *trunk* that carries water up from the *roots* to the rest of the tree.

scales (1) The tough, woody parts of a *cone* (2) A *bud*'s outer layers.

seed Grows from a fertilized *ovule*, and may eventually form a new plant.

seedling A very young tree that has grown from a *seed*.

sepals Leaf-like parts that protect *buds*.

shoot A young stem or twig bearing leaves.

simple leaf A type of leaf that is all in one piece.

stamen The male part of a *flower*, where *pollen* is made.

terminal bud A *bud* at the tip of a shoot or twig.

timber Wood, especially when harvested.

toothed leaf A leaf or *leaflet* with jagged edges.

trunk The main woody stem of the tree that holds it upright.

variegated A type of leaf that has two or more colours.

veins Tiny tubes inside a leaf that carry water to all parts of the leaf and carry food away from it.

Acorns ripening on an English oak tree

Wild Flowers

Wild flowers in
a hay meadow

Here are some of the places where wild flowers grow.

Rosebay willowherb grows at the side of railways.

White campion can be found in hedgerows.

Look for brooklime in marshes and by rivers.

Here are some of the many wild flowers you might spot growing on waste ground or in a country meadow.

Flowers in the wild

With their flimsy petals and delicate stalks, wild flowers like poppies and daisies may seem rather fragile. As a group of plants, though, they are really very tough. There have been flowering plants on Earth for over 145 million years, which makes flowers some of the best survivors on the planet. They can grow almost anywhere: from the hottest deserts to the coldest mountains and the dirtiest cities.

Originally, all flowers were wild; they just grew wherever they could. But, over time, people began to realize how useful flowers were, so they started growing them on purpose – for their looks, smell, taste, and to use as medicines. All the flowers people grow today have wild ancestors.

Field scabious

Hawkbit

Wild carrot

Looking for wild flowers

You're likely to see the widest variety of wild flowers in grassy, natural areas, but once you start looking, you may be surprised where they spring up. Most flowers need certain conditions to grow well. A plant's home, or habitat, provides all the things it needs to survive. Some flowers can grow almost anywhere. Others are fussier, so you'll only find them in certain places.

Yellow archangel is common in woods.

Sand dunes and cliffs are the best places to look for stonecrop.

Watercress usually grows in fast-flowing, chalky streams.

Shepherd's purse will grow pretty much anywhere.

Clumps of sea kale grow on pebbly beaches.

In the wild, flowers live and die at their own pace, and make seeds so new flowers can grow. If you pick them, though, there'll be fewer seeds, then fewer flowers – and some may disappear altogether. So look, but don't pick, and there'll always be wild flowers for everyone to enjoy.

Common butterwort can be found on mountains.

Greater knapweed

How a flower grows

A flower goes through several very different stages during its life. You might see young undeveloped flowers, curled up inside a bud, or others which have stopped flowering and turned into fruits and seeds.

Here you can see the life story of a poppy. All flowers (well, almost all) develop in a similar way.

Bud

1. A poppy plant grows from a seed. Buds form, with flowers curled up inside.

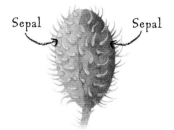

Sepal   Sepal

2. Leaf-like sepals protect the delicate petals. They begin to open as the flower grows.

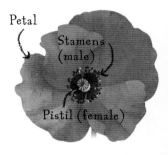

Petal   Stamens (male)   Pistil (female)

3. Inside the petals are male and female parts called the stamens and pistil.

Stigma   Ovary

4. The pistil is made of two parts: a sticky stigma on top and an ovary beneath.

Anther

5. Pod-like anthers on the tips of the stamens make a powder, called pollen.

6. A bee visits the poppy to feed. Pollen sticks to the bee, who takes it to another poppy.

This pistil is shown cut in half.

Pollen grain

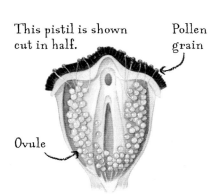

Ovule

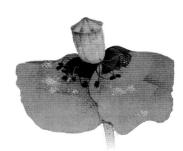

7. The pollen rubs off onto a poppy's stigma. Tubes grow from the pollen down to egg-like ovules inside the ovary.

8. Pollen has tiny bits inside, which travel down the tubes into the ovules. The stamens and petals wilt and drop off.

9. Inside the pistil, the ovules start turning into seeds. The pistil swells, and is now called a fruit.

Hole

Seeds

10. The fruit ripens and its wall dries up. When the wind blows, the seeds are shaken out of holes, like pepper from a pot.

To make seeds, these poppies must have pollen from other poppies. Pollen from any other flowers just won't do.

Most wild flowers have the same basic bits and pieces, but they can look very different from each other.

How plants live

Flowers are a plant's seed factories, making seeds that will grow into new plants. Other parts do different jobs to keep the plant alive.

During the day, leaves make food, using water, and a gas called carbon dioxide from the air. To do this, they need energy, which they absorb from sunlight. The stem is a plant's transport system. It has bundles of tubes inside that carry food and water to every part. Hidden underground, roots are busy too, taking water and goodness from the soil and fixing the plant to the spot.

Rosebay willowherb

Flower

Leaf

Stem

Roots

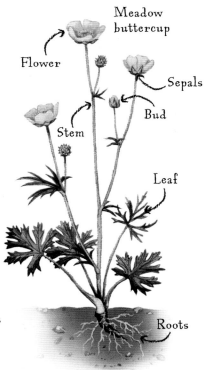

Meadow buttercup

Flower

Stem

Sepals

Bud

Leaf

Roots

Buds have undeveloped flowers or leaves inside. Flower buds are protected by leaf-like sepals.

The stem carries water from the roots to the leaves, and carries food from the leaves to the rest of the plant.

As well as making food, leaves take in gases from the air and release gases and water that the plant doesn't need.

The mesh of roots anchors the plant in the ground, stopping it from being blown or washed away.

Flower field guides

You probably know the names of more wild flowers than you think. Try writing down all the ones you know, and see how many you get. To identify the names of flowers you don't know, you'll need a flower field guide. Here's the sort of information you'll find in a typical flower identification guide.

Many flower guides show a full-length picture of the flowering plant, and a close-up of its flower, too.

COMMON POPPY

Species: *Papaver rhoeas*
Family: *Papaveraceae*
In flower: Summer
Habitat: Fields and meadows

Each flower has a scientific name in Latin. This might not be the name you know it by.

This is where the flower usually grows in the wild.

Seed pods develop in late summer.

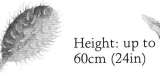

Buds covered in small spikes

Height: up to 60cm (24in)

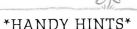

HANDY HINTS

To help you choose a flower guide, look up a flower you already know:
• Is it easy to find?
• Does the picture look like the flower?
• Are the words easy to read?
• Does it tell you what you want to know?

There are lots of flower identification guides to choose from. To help you begin spotting wild flowers straight away. You can find a short one at the end of this of this section, starting on page 214.

How to identify flowers

There are thousands and thousands of different wild flowers. That may seem a bit daunting, but if you look for the most obvious features, you'll soon learn to recognize the most common ones. The more you notice about a plant, the easier it'll be to look up. In your guide, the colour, size and shape of petals and sepals hold the biggest clues.

Each cornflower stem has a single flower head.

The petals of this Lady's bedstraw make a cross shape.

Wood anemones are shaped like stars.

Each early purple orchid stem has several flowers growing around it.

Harebells are named after their bell-shaped flowers.

Greater bindweed flowers are trumpet shaped.

Meadowsweet has clusters of small flowers.

The hood is called a standard.

The lip is called a keel.

The petals of rest harrow flowers form a hood and lips.

Spur

Larkspur flowers form a tube called a spur.

Looking at leaves

Leaves can help you identify a plant, too. Do they have one overall shape or does each stalk have several leafy parts, known as leaflets? Do these look hairy or bumpy, smooth or spiky? Colours range from dull grey, red and purple, to bronze, silver and gold, as well as almost every imaginable shade of green.

Lesser celandine has heart-shaped leaves.

The leaves of brooklime are oval with toothed edges.

Lobe

White bryony has lobed leaves.

Common centaury leaves are smooth and narrow.

Sea holly has prickly silvery blue-green leaves.

Each Alpine milk vetch leaf is made up of smaller leaflets.

LEAF ARRANGEMENTS

Here are a few of the different ways that leaves can be arranged on a stem.

Sand spurrey leaves grow along the stems in opposite pairs.

Leaves of white helleborine sit alternately along the stem.

Ice plant leaves grow in spirals up the stem.

Rosettes of primrose leaves grow around the base of the stem.

Wild flower calendar

Most flowers bloom in spring and summer, but some wait until autumn before opening their petals. A few even thrive in the icy frost and snow of winter. This calendar shows you just a few of the flowers you might see if you go out spotting in different seasons.

Winter

Snowdrop

Winter aconite

Butterbur

Daisy

Spring

Wild daffodil

Greater stitchwort

Primrose

Bird's-foot trefoil

Wood anemone

Common dog violet

Cowslip

Sweet violet

Summer

Snapdragon

Purple loosestrife

Red campion

Enchanter's nightshade

Meadowsweet

Sweet William

Blackberry

Musk mallow

Larkspur

Dog rose

Bats-in-the-belfry

Yellow pimpernel

Autumn

Soapwort

Field scabious

Autumn crocus

Autumn feltwort

Keeping a flower diary

You could try keeping a record of flowers you've seen. Start by making rough notes and sketches of flowers when you're out and about. At the end of a trip, you could copy them into a flower diary, noting when and where you saw the flowers. You could include drawings, photos and leaf rubbings, too. As you add to your diary over the year, you'll also build up a picture of how plants change with the seasons.

You could decorate your diary with pressed flowers.

SPOTTING TIP

Useful things to take on a flower spotting trip:
• Notepad (spiral bound ones are best)
• Pencils
• Tape measure
• Camera
• Magnifying glass

July 12th

Stour Meadows
Warm and sunny

Golden flowers, flat on top

Flowers are 20mm across.

Flowers look like daisies.

Spear-shaped leaves

Hairy stem

Plant is 40cm high.

Wavy edges

Common fleabane

Pressing flowers

You can press flowers to stick in your diary or to decorate cards, notepaper, bookmarks and gift tags. Only use garden or bought flowers, though, not ones growing in the wild.

1. Pick some clean, dry, fully opened flowers. Choose flowers that are naturally flat, such as violas, petunias and primulas.

2. Lay a piece of blotting paper on one page of an old book. Put the flowers on the paper and lay another piece of paper over them.

3. Close the book and stack more books on top. Leave the flowers there for at least two weeks until they're dry and flat.

Rubbing leaves

Rubbing leaves makes prints of their shapes and the pattern on their surface. You could make leaf rubbings in your notebook or, like pressed flowers, use them to decorate things.

Your rubbing will show up the patterns on the leaf.

1. Find a clean, dry, flat leaf and put it on a piece of paper.

2. Place more paper on top. Rub gently over it with a crayon or pencil.

You could arrange a few leaves in a group before rubbing them.

171

These wild flowers
are easy to grow.

Knapweed

Bugle

Flower

Field
scabious

Growing wild flowers

One of the best ways to watch wild flowers
change is to grow some of your own from
seeds. You can buy these from garden centres
and nurseries. Some packets contain mixed wild
flower seeds; others have just one kind. If
you're growing plants that usually flower in
summer, start growing the seeds indoors, in
early spring. Then, when they've grown into
baby plants (seedlings, in plant-speak), you can
move them outside, once the weather's warm.

Cornflowers like these
are becoming rare in
the wild, but you can
grow your own from
a packet of seeds.

How to grow wild flowers

To grow some wild flowers, you will need: a seed tray with holes in the bottom; compost; wild flower seeds; trowel; dibber or stick; watering can; plastic food wrap; several 7cm (3in) pots; three or more 15cm (6in) pots.

Push the seeds with your finger.

1. Fill the tray with compost to 2cm (1in) below the rim. Sow the seeds following the instructions on the packet.

2. Scatter compost on top. Stretch food wrap over the tray. Keep it in a light place until green shoots appear.

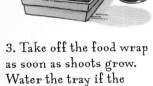

Check how damp the compost is every day.

3. Take off the food wrap as soon as shoots grow. Water the tray if the compost feels dry when you press the top.

Pick the seedlings that look most healthy.

4. Half fill the small pots with compost. Push the dibber or stick into the soil by a seedling and lift up its roots and soil.

Hold onto the lower leaves as you lift.

5. Hold the seedling in a pot. Fill in around it with compost. Do the same for each seedling. Keep the pots inside.

6. After a few weeks, if the weather is warm, partly fill the bigger pots with compost, as shown here.

Tap the bottom of the pot.

7. Put a finger on either side of the stem of the healthiest looking plant. Turn its pot over and tip the seedling and compost out.

8. Hold the plant by its stem and put it in a big pot. Fill compost around it. Do the same for a few more plants. Place the pots outside.

These flowers are especially attractive to butterflies.

Candytuft

Michaelmas daisy

Willow gentian

This flat, orange flower makes a handy landing pad for lots of insects, including butterflies.

Showing off

Many flowers make a sweet, syrupy liquid called nectar to attract insects. Some insects eat pollen, too. The shape and colour of their petals often advertises these tasty treats, just as attractive shop window displays tempt customers inside. In spring and summer, look for insects feeding on flowers, and see if you can spot which ones go where.

Insects keep a look out for flowers that will be convenient for them to feed from. Those with short mouthparts, such as bees and flies, tend to prefer flowers with a shallow saucer, star, or cross shape. But flowers shaped like trumpets, funnels or long cups are better suited to moths and butterflies. This is because they have long, curly tongues that can reach down to the nectar at the bottom of the petals.

Seeing signals

Insects see colours differently from people, and are drawn to colours that stand out the most to them. For example, bees are often attracted to yellow and blue flowers, while butterflies tend to flit towards pinks, reds and oranges. Moths – which fly around at night – visit white and cream flowers, because they're easier to see in the dark.

To a person, an evening primrose looks plain creamy-yellow...

...but, to a bee, it looks blue with vivid stripes and patches in the middle.

The dots on these foxgloves guide bees as they crawl inside to get to the nectar.

The reason bees see things differently is because they can sense ultraviolet light, a type of light that's invisible to people. This enables them to see marks that other creatures can't. These marks form patterns that lead them to the heart of the flower, where nectar is made – a bit like airport runway lights showing pilots where to land.

Some petals have nectar guides that you can see, too. How many different examples of stripes, splodges and spots can you find?

DID YOU KNOW?

In some countries, birds, bats, mice, and even monkeys drink nectar and eat pollen from wild flowers.

A snapdragon's smell is made up of just seven different oils...

...while an orchid has 100 oils to make its scent.

Making scents

When you're out and about spotting flowers, you'll notice that many of them have a nice smell. This comes from oils in their petals, sepals, pollen or nectar. For thousands of years, people have used flower petals to scent their homes, and have made them into perfumes to make themselves smell sweet, too.

But flowers don't just smell good to please people. Their scented oils are a signal to insects, usually to let them know that they have a tasty supply of pollen and nectar to feed on. Each type of flower has a different combination of oils to make its own, distinctive smell – anything from seven to as many as a hundred different oils.

Lavender has a strong, sweet scent that attracts bees and butterflies.

Day scents

Not all perfumed flowers smell 24 hours a day. Some turn off their scents at night by folding up their petals to protect their insides from the cold, and early morning dew. Insects can't feed when the flowers are closed, so the flowers don't release their oils then. But, in the morning, they unfold their petals and let their fragrance waft out, telling insects that they're open for business again.

These flowers are scented only during the day.

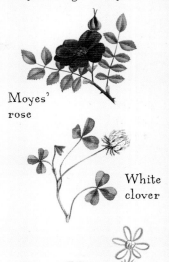

Moyes'
rose

White
clover

A Pasque flower closes at night.

In the morning, it opens up again to tempt insects with its scent and colour.

DID YOU KNOW?
Some types of evening primrose burst open so quickly at night that they make a popping sound.

Night scents

Some flowers are open all the time, but don't smell very strongly until night falls. Then, they release heavily-scented oils to attract moths and other night insects. Other flowers wait until night before they open at all. Night-scented flowers usually smell more strongly than day-scented ones, to help insects find them in the dark.

Peach
blossom
moth

Honeysuckle is especially strongly scented at night.

Pollen-movers

The reason why flowers do so much to attract insects – using their shape, colour and smell – is because they need the insects to move their pollen to another flower of the same kind. This is the only way for most flowers to make seeds, which will grow into new plants. Many types of plant would die out completely if insects didn't do this vital job for them.

Insects don't move pollen on purpose, though – it happens by accident as they fly from flower to flower in search of food.

DID YOU KNOW?

If you see a striped, hairy insect feeding from a flower, it might be a bee – but it might not. Some flies that drink nectar look a lot like bees. You can tell the difference by counting their wings. Bees have four, but flies only have two.

Hover fly

Drone fly

Large wing

Small wing

Honey bee, with two pairs of wings

1. As a bee drinks from a meadow clary flower, its body gets covered in pollen.

2. The bee flies to another flower, carrying the first flower's pollen on its body.

3. The pollen brushes off the bee's body, onto the flower's stigma.

4. As the bee takes another drink, it gets dusted with new pollen, and off it goes again...

The pale specks you can see on this bee's hairy body are grains of lavender pollen.

Sticking on

It can be a risky journey for a grain of hitchhiking pollen. It has to avoid being blown away as its pilot flies through the air, or being brushed off as its chauffeur creeps along the ground. Some pollen is sticky or spiky, so it can fix itself onto an insect. Some flowers, such as many orchids, go one step further by packing their pollen into waxy bags that clip onto insects' heads as they feed.

Tiny yellow powder-filled packages of orchid pollen stick to bee's heads.

DID YOU KNOW?

Slugs and snails are slow but steady pollen-movers. As they slither and slide from one flower to another, they ooze thick slime, which pollen sticks to.

Most insects that feed from flowers, such as bees, wasps and butterflies, have tiny hairs on their bodies. The bees brush past the stamens as they push into the flowers to reach the nectar, and the sticky pollen clings to their hairs.

Pollen from these flowers blows away on the wind.

Pigweed pollen

Nettle pollen

Broad-leaved dock pollen

Pollen in the air

Not all flowers need insects to carry pollen for them – some let their pollen blow away on the wind. Just as spiky or sticky pollen is well-designed for latching onto passing insects, so wind-spread pollen is ideally shaped for catching the lightest breeze. Ragweeds, for instance, have grains of round, dimpled pollen that soar through the air like mini golf balls.

The pollen of most grasses and trees is spread in this way. It's this airborne pollen that gives some people hayfever in the spring and summer, making them sniff and sneeze.

The yellow blobs on these hare's tail flowers are stamens covered in pollen.

Catching the wind

To flowers whose pollen is spread by air, being brightly coloured or deliciously scented isn't important. Their aim is to catch the wind – not to attract visitors – so their small, light pollen needs to be easily accessible.

   You can often tell which flowers use the wind to spread pollen because their stamens are literally hanging around, waiting for a breeze. The further they dangle, the better, so each gust can catch as much pollen as possible.

Ribwort plantain

Hoary plantain

Greater plantain

These flowers have stamens that hang out, exposed to any passing breath of air.

Doing it for themselves

To grow seeds, most flowers need pollen from another flower of the same type. But a few can manage perfectly well without – they can use their own. When pollen drops from their stamens onto their stigmas, seeds start to grow. If their pollen hasn't dropped (or been carried away by visitors), some flowers can even move it themselves.

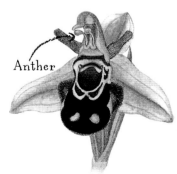

Anther

A bee orchid moves pollen by bending its anthers down towards its stigma, which is inside the lower petal.

The upper petal of this broom flower keeps the rain off its pollen.

When a bee lands on the lower petal, it bends, exposing the stamens.

Protecting pollen

Grains of pollen are fragile and can easily be washed away by rain or dew, or damaged by extreme temperatures. It's a flower's job to protect its precious pollen from these dangers.

Sheltering shapes

A flower's shape affects how much protection it can offer. When it's raining, you might see raindrops trickling down the petals of bell- or umbrella-shaped flowers. These drooping flowers make a good shelter for pollen, as water can't collect inside them.

Some flowers have petals that act like umbrellas – the rain rolls right off them.

Snowdrops

Bluebells

The petals of some flowers, such as broom and snapdragons, form hinged pouches. Most of the time they're firmly closed, with their powdery treasure safe inside. When an insect lands, they open up – but only if it's big and heavy enough to prise open the flowery jaws.

Moving petals

Some flowers protect their pollen by only opening their petals when the weather is warm and sunny. If the temperature drops, the petals close and the pollen stays safe.

Many flowers have regular opening and closing times, spreading their petals after dawn and folding them away again at dusk. This protects their pollen from the lowest temperatures and from the damp droplets of morning dew and evening mist.

Some Pasque flowers bend their stalks in the rain, so the flowers hang down like bells rather than sitting upright like cups.

Morning glory gets its name from its habit of opening during the day.

Daisies open their petals in the day and close them at night.

Open flowers

Closed flowers

TRY THIS

Flowers can tell if it's dark or light. To see this for yourself, put two house plants of the same type, both with open flowers, on a sunny windowsill. Cover one with a box to block out the light. Leave them for a few hours, then lift up the box. What do you see?

Flower   Fruit

Sorrel fruits can be carried away on the wind.

Flower   Fruit

Red campion seeds grow in pods and are shaken out by the wind.

Flower   Fruit

Dandelion fruits have white, silky "parachutes" that catch the wind.

Flower   Fruit

A sea rocket seed pod drops into the water, and opens to let its seeds float away.

Fruits and seeds

Once flowers' stigmas have the pollen they need, new life begins. The ovaries turn into fruits and, hidden inside them, tiny ovules slowly ripen into seeds. When a seed is ripe and ready, it needs to find a place of its own, with enough space and light for it to grow into a flower. If a fruit just falls to the ground, the seed will be in the shadow of its parent, and won't be able to grow properly. So the further away it can move, the better.

Floating and sailing

Looking closely at seeds or fruits can sometimes give you a clue as to how they might have travelled. Some have hairs or wings, that help them catch the wind. Some don't need flying equipment at all – they're so small and light that the slightest breeze can carry them away.

For fruits that grow in or near water, spreading seeds can be as easy as letting them drop down and sail away. The seeds are often light enough to float, and have a coating to protect them from water damage. Sometimes the whole fruit drops into the water before opening up to release its seeds.

Popping out

Some seeds explode into the world. Either their fruits burst open, or the threads that attach them to the fruit suddenly snap, and they shoot into the air.

A herb Robert seed pod opens with a sudden spring action and flings its seeds into the air.

Hitching a ride

If you see a seed or fruit that's covered in tiny hooks, it's probably a hitchhiker. The hooks catch onto the fur of passing animals, or cling to people's clothes as they brush past. The seed is carried away and eventually falls off.

Agrimony fruits have hooks that latch onto fur or clothing.

Animals also help spread seeds by eating them. As they munch on fruit, they either drop the seeds onto the ground or swallow them. Swallowed seeds pass through animals undamaged and come out in their droppings.

By eating these blackberries, this squirrel is helping spread seeds.

These wild flowers
grow from bulbs.

Winter aconite

Lesser celandine

Wild daffodil

New plants from old

When it comes to making new plants, many
wild flowers don't leave anything to chance.
After a chilly summer, with fewer insects,
their whole future could be in peril. So, as
well as making pollen, flowers often have
other cunning ways of producing offspring.

Underground larders

As winter approaches, some old, dying plants
form a food store called a bulb or a corm. A bulb
is a type of scaly underground stem, like a tiny
onion. It contains food, layers of leaves and the
beginnings of a new stem and roots.

Corms are similar, but without the layers.
When its time's up, the plant above the ground
dies away. But, hidden below, the store stays alive
and, in the next year, a fresh, new plant emerges.

Each of these spring
crocuses has grown
from a corm below
the ground.

Honeysuckle makes seeds but can also grow from stems called runners.

Keep on running

Some plants grow long side stems called runners. When a runner touches the ground, it develops roots of its own and starts to grow into a new plant. At first, the parent plant sends food through the runner to its offspring. But, once it can live on its own, the runner rots away and the new plant is left to fend for itself.

Silverweed develops red, hairy runners.

Strawberry plant

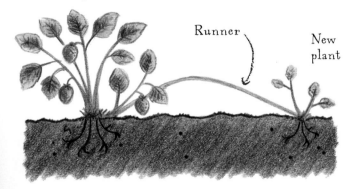

Runner

New plant

Soapwort can grow from seeds or rhizomes.

Rhizomes are thick underground runners that grow out sideways from a plant's roots. New roots sprout from the bottom of a rhizome, and shoots grow from knobbly buds on top. Roots and buds can grow at any point along it. So, with the help of one rhizome, a plant can quickly and stealthily take over a wide area. Mint and most grasses spread this way.

Greater bindweed spreads rapidly however it can – by seeds, runners or rhizomes.

Look out for these plants
that live less than a year.

Love lies
bleeding

Corn cockle

Red campion

Ivy-
leaved
toadflax

How long do flowers live?

Even the toughest plants can't live for ever
and each plant has its own natural lifespan,
which is the time it takes to grow, flower,
develop fruit and spread seeds. Some plants
do these things once in their lives; others
repeat them year after year. Once a plant
has come to the end of its lifespan, it dies.

One year...

Plants that only last a single year are called
annuals. Some go from a seed to a dead plant
in just a few months. Annuals usually grow
and flower during the spring, develop fruit in
the summer and die by the end of autumn.
Their seeds lie resting over winter, ready to
grow into new flowers the following spring.

...or two?

Biennial plants last for two years. In their first
year, they grow and store food. In the second,
they flower, make seeds and die.
Their seeds grow into new
flowers the following year.

Viper's bugloss spends one year
growing and storing food. The
next year it flowers, makes and
spreads seeds, then dies.

Long-lasting plants

Some plants can live for years, growing and flowering every spring. These are called perennials. In winter, some or all of the parts that are above the ground wither away, but the roots remain alive, using up food stored in them over spring and summer. When spring comes again, a new flower grows from these roots.

Unexpected flowers

The most unpredictable kinds of plant are called ephemerals. You may not see anything of an ephemeral plant for months, or even years. Then, as soon as the plant has the growing conditions it needs, it will quickly grow, flower, develop seeds and die. Depending on the plant, this whole cycle can be over in less than a month.

These plants can live for many years.

Bloody crane's-bill

Anemone

Chickweed seeds can lie resting in an unused field for years and years, but spring to life when the field is ploughed.

Secrets of survival

A plant's life is not an easy one. If it manages to survive the heat and cold, flood and drought, it still has to escape creatures that want to eat it. Plants may not be able to run, but many still have ways to dodge predators, call for help, hide and even fight back. What's more amazing is that you usually won't be able to tell when it's happening: most plants do all this without moving a millimetre.

Stinging and scratching

If you look closely, you'll see that some plants have stiff spines, sharp thorns, pointy prickles or stinging hairs growing on them. These are there to put animals off eating them – the plant's way of saying, "Leave me alone!" It tells them that chewing and swallowing it would be painful.

Rough poppy stems are hairy and their sepals are covered in bristles.

Blackberry stems are thorny.

Common teasels are covered in sturdy spines.

Scents and poisons

Some plants can call for help by releasing scents into the air. When cabbage white caterpillars take their first nibble of a wild cabbage leaf, the plant lets rip with an unusual smell. This is picked up by braconid wasps, which eat cabbage white caterpillars. They know that if they follow the scent, they'll soon find a juicy snack.

Many plants defend themselves by making poisonous chemicals in their leaves when they're being eaten. Some give off these poisons in their scent too, so any passing animals know to leave them alone.

Wild cabbage flowers can make a special smell to call for help in emergencies.

These flowers are all poisonous.

Black nightshade   Yellow iris   Ragwort

Buttercup   Pellitory-of-the-wall   Autumn crocus

DID YOU KNOW?

Monkshood is one of the most poisonous flowering plants. Eating any part of it can cause serious illnesses or even death.

191

Sweet violet flowers are used to flavour desserts.

Rape seeds are squeezed to get cooking oil out of them.

Broom flowers make a yellow dye.

Using flowers

Flowers come in such a range of colours and shapes that people all over the world use them as decorations in their homes and gardens, and as symbols in celebrations and religious ceremonies. But flowers aren't just pretty to look at – for centuries, people have been discovering plenty of practical uses for them, too.

Cooking and colouring

Have you ever eaten a flower? Using flowers in cooking isn't as unusual as you might think. Parts of flowering plants, such as petals, leaves and roots are used to flavour food. Some petals can even be eaten raw and rose petals give Turkish delight its colour and taste. Lots of flowers, including jasmine, rose, chamomile, cowslip and comfrey, are used to make tea.

Cowslip

Boiling flowers is also a good way to make dyes. Lots of flowers, such as barberry, broom and ragwort, will colour the water they are boiled in. That water can then be used to dye fabric or even hair. It's not just petals that make dyes; brilliant colours can be extracted from roots, berries and leaves, too.

192

Medicines

Throughout history, plants have been used as medicines, to treat everything from colds to cholera. Today, people still use natural remedies, such as tea made from ginger to cure a sore throat or an upset stomach. Scientists use plants as ingredients in modern medicines, too. Foxgloves, for example, are used to make digoxin, a drug to treat heart disease.

Lavender and chamomile lotions can be used to treat burns, boils and insect bites.

Flowery fragrances

Scents from sweet-smelling flowers can be extracted to make perfume. This is done by boiling the flowers, cooling the steam and collecting droplets of scented oil from it. Thousands of petals are needed to make a tiny amount of the oil, so perfumes made with pure flower oil are very expensive. Most perfume-makers use chemicals instead.

The scented oils of lily-of-the-valley are extracted and used to make sweet, light perfumes.

DID YOU KNOW?

People have been making perfume for thousands of years. To make themselves smell nice, Ancient Egyptians soaked petals in fat, and moulded it into cones to put on their heads.

Look out for these flowers
in walls and pavements.

Yarrow

Purslane

Houseleek

Towns and cities

Towns might not seem the most promising
places to start a wild flower search, but if
you keep your eyes peeled, you'll see them all
around. Look in streets and car parks, waste
ground and building sites, parks, gardens and
churchyards. You'll often find flowers growing
in unlikely places: in between paving stones,
in walls, even in cracks in buildings –
anywhere where they can find enough soil.

Most of these flowers are weeds – plants
that grow where they're not wanted – and
their seeds are usually spread by the wind.

Wallflowers are garden
flowers but they often
escape into the wild.

Pellitory-
of-the-wall

Prickly
sow thistle

Ivy-leaved toadflax

Shepherd's
purse

Dandelion

Ribwort
plantain

White
clover

Weeds

Some weeds behave like vandals, tearing up road surfaces and widening cracks in pipes and walls. They're a quick-spreading menace in gardens, using water and light needed by plants that gardeners work so hard to grow. Others do no harm, though, and some can even be useful, providing birds and insects with food and a safe place to lay their eggs.

DID YOU KNOW?

Oxford ragwort grows well in building sites and by railways, where it's dusty and dry. It originally grew on the parched, ashy sides of Mount Etna, a volcano in Italy.

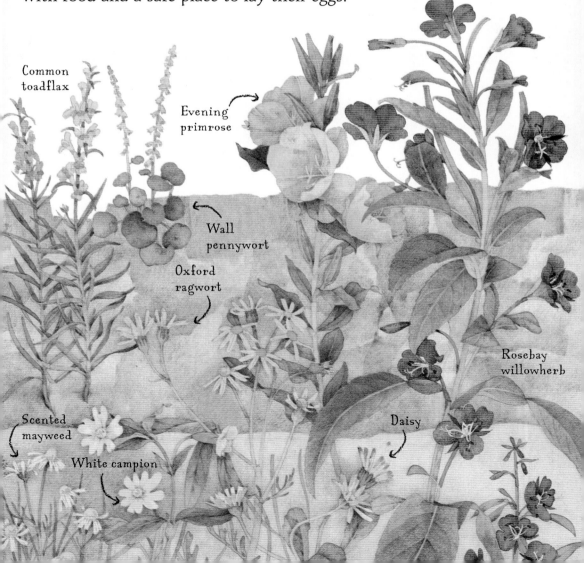

Common toadflax

Evening primrose

Wall pennywort

Oxford ragwort

Rosebay willowherb

Scented mayweed

Daisy

White campion

Hedgerows

Dog rose

When you set off into the country in search of wild flowers, probably the first things you'll come across are hedgerows. These bushes and banks shelter the sides of roads and fields and provide a safe home for all sorts of wild flowers.

Wild clematis

High branches screen them from cold and stormy weather, blocking gusty winds, and catching flurries of snow in winter. Fallen autumn leaves blanket the ground underneath, protecting flowers from frost. As they rot, they release nutrients into the soil too, making it rich and nourishing.

Cow parsley

Honeysuckle

Hedgerows are full of life, providing food and shelter for different kinds of wild flowers, birds and animals.

Common teasel

Stinging nettle

Foxglove

Survival challenge

With all these benefits, it's hardly surprising that hedgerows are so popular. In fact, overcrowding is often a problem and each plant has to struggle for space to grow.

The tall hedges that make such efficient windbreaks can also block out the sun and rain. In their shadow, competition for sunlight and water can be fierce. Many flowers survive by climbing – clinging to branches for support as they scramble up towards the light. Meanwhile, in the soil below, the battle for water is fought unseen, as tangled roots stretch and strain to soak up every last drop.

Even visits from animals that will move pollen or spread seeds can't be taken for granted. Flowers fill the hedgerows with bright, richly scented displays of petals or fruits as they vie for their attention.

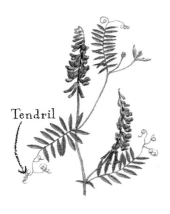

Dog roses use their sharp thorns to grip onto other plants, as they climb up to reach the light.

Tendril

Tufted vetch winds its curly tendrils around hedge branches.

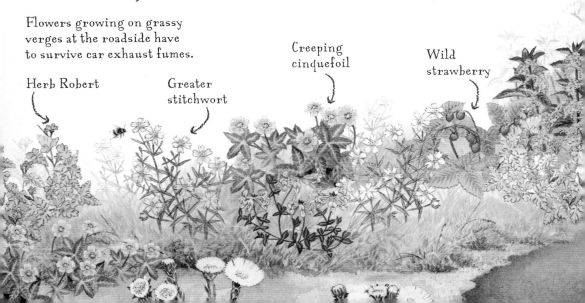

Flowers growing on grassy verges at the roadside have to survive car exhaust fumes.

Creeping cinquefoil

Wild strawberry

Herb Robert

Greater stitchwort

These flowers are common in fields and meadows.

Oxeye daisy

Hogweed

Bird's-foot trefoil

Creeping buttercup

Fields and meadows

Nothing may seem more natural than grassy pastures full of wild flowers. But it's the fact that they're regularly mown, by machines or the chomping teeth of hungry animals, that allows such a wide variety to survive. If they weren't cut back, the stronger species would rampage across the fields, and smother the weaker flowers out of existence.

Wild flowers spring up in crops, too. Farmers sometimes regard them as weeds, because they take valuable space, water and food away from crops, or poison livestock. Some farmers get rid of them by digging them up or spraying them with chemicals. Flowers are also harmed indirectly by chemicals used to kill pests, which often kill pollen-movers, too.

Next time you're in a field or meadow, try counting how many kinds of wild flowers you can spot.

Meadow thistle

Common comfrey

Red clover

Protecting wildlife

Recently, many farmers have started setting aside strips at the edges of fields, or even whole fields, where wildlife can thrive. Some also use ways to control weeds and pests that don't do such widespread damage to other plant or insect communities. Here are three flowers to look out for in wild areas on farmland.

Cornflower

Corn spurrey

Snake's head fritillary

Meadowsweet

Yellow rattle

Common valerian

Wild pansy

Oak
leaves

Oak fruit
(acorns)
in autumn

Oak woods

In oak woods in spring, you may be lucky enough to find spectacular carpets of flowers such as primroses and bluebells. At this time of year, growing conditions are good. The soil is rich with decaying leaves, trees give protection from the wind and, while the branches are still bare, there's plenty of light.

In summer, it's a different story. The woods are darker, as the leafy canopy shades the woodland floor, so you'll find most flowers in clearings or by paths. Some light still filters through, though, and a few flowers can thrive in the dappled light.

Spring and early summer
are the best times for
spotting flowers
in oak woods.

Look for these flowers growing
in oak woods in spring.

Primrose   Wood anemone   Lesser periwinkle   Wood sorrel

In summer, you might find these
flowers in an oak wood.

Foxglove   Red campion   Enchanter's nightshade   Wood woundwort

Beech leaves

Beech fruit (in autumn)

SPOTTING TIP

It's hard for flowers to grow in conifer woods, because the trees have leaves on them all year round. You're most likely to find flowers in summer, in areas where trees have been cut down.

Norway spruce tree

Beech woods

Flowers that grow in beech woods prefer thin soil that doesn't hold much water. Like oaks, beeches shed their leaves each autumn, but the leaves break down so slowly that a thick layer of leaf litter covers the ground all year. Plant seedlings struggle to push through these dead leaves to the light.

You'll find the most flowers in areas with the fewest trees, for example along paths and by streams. In spring, look out for carpets of bluebells in clearings or at the edges of the woods. In summer, the leaves form a dense canopy, which blocks the sunlight, casting deep shadows. Only a few flowers can grow in the dim light of a beechwood summer.

The leafy branches of these closely growing beech trees prevent much light from reaching the forest floor.

Here are some flowers you might
see in beech woods in spring.

Common dog violet

Arum

Sweet woodruff

Bluebell

These flowers grow in beech
woods during the summer.

Bats-in-the-belfry

Golden rod

Red helleborine

Wood avens

Little air pockets in duckweed plants enable them to float on the water's surface.

Flowers

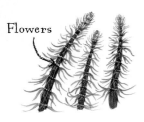

Mare's tails can grow completely under water. They have tiny green flowers with no petals.

Ponds and streams

Plants can flourish in a range of watery habitats, from cool, green ponds to clear, tumbling streams or fast-flowing rivers. But water isn't the most stable of environments. Heavy rains might fill a pond to overflowing, and then a dry spell might shrink it to a puddle. Even a light breeze sends ripples racing over the surface. So plants have adapted in ingenious ways.

Some have roots that reach right down, anchoring them in the soft mud. Their long, flexible stems allow the flowers to float on the surface, whether the water rises or falls. Other plants just drift around, absorbing nutrients from the water through their trailing roots.

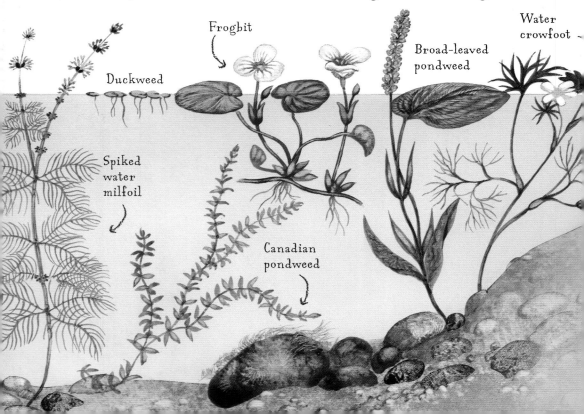

Frogbit

Duckweed

Water crowfoot

Broad-leaved pondweed

Spiked water milfoil

Canadian pondweed

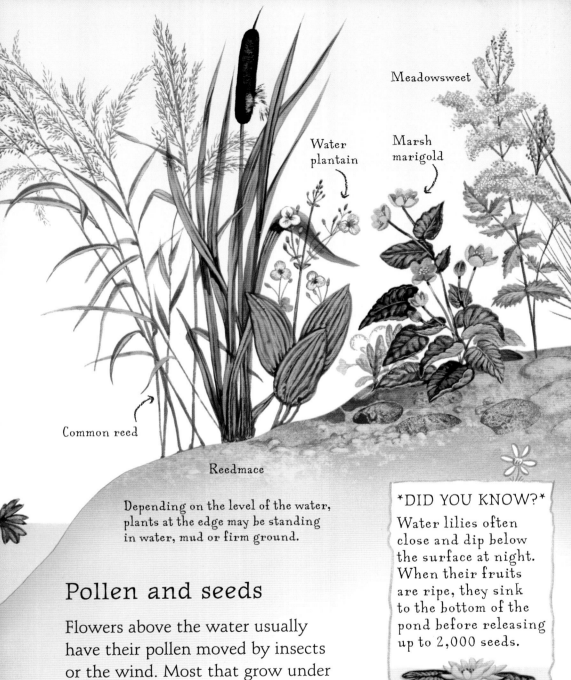

Meadowsweet

Water
plantain

Marsh
marigold

Common reed

Reedmace

Depending on the level of the water,
plants at the edge may be standing
in water, mud or firm ground.

Pollen and seeds

Flowers above the water usually
have their pollen moved by insects
or the wind. Most that grow under
the surface release their pollen into
the water and it floats away. When
they develop into fruits, the seeds
are spread in the same way.

DID YOU KNOW?
Water lilies often
close and dip below
the surface at night.
When their fruits
are ripe, they sink
to the bottom of the
pond before releasing
up to 2,000 seeds.

Flexible
stem

By the seashore

Sunny weather, sea breezes and salty air make coasts popular spots for tourists, but, for the plants that live there, life's a constant battle for survival. Strong sea winds can easily uproot plants that are too tall or aren't anchored firmly enough to the ground.

Golden samphire   Sea pea   Shrubby seablite

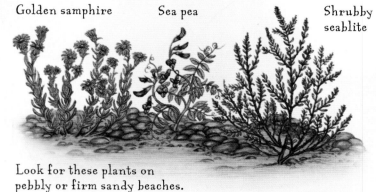

Look for these plants on pebbly or firm sandy beaches.

Some plants can be found on the beach itself. They have long, sprawling roots to hold them fast while the sand and pebbles shift with the tides. Roots also need to go deep for fresh water and nutrients.

Sea rocket

Sea lyme grass   Sea couch grass   Marram grass

Sea sandwort

Saving water

You might think plants near the sea have more than enough water, but they're actually always in danger of drying out. Sea water is too salty to use, and strong, salty breezes and bright sunshine can soon wither plants unless they find ways to protect the water inside them.

The leaves of these plants help them save water in different ways.

The hairy leaves of yellow horned poppies catch drops of dew and rain.

Sand dunes

The best spots for survival are where there's shelter from the wind, sea and sun. Low sandy hills, called dunes, can offer exactly this. Most flowers grow on the side facing away from the sea, often forming creeping mats on the ground, where they're less exposed to strong winds.

Sea holly leaves have a thick, waxy skin to keep the water in.

Sand dunes offer plants welcome areas of protection from strong sea winds.

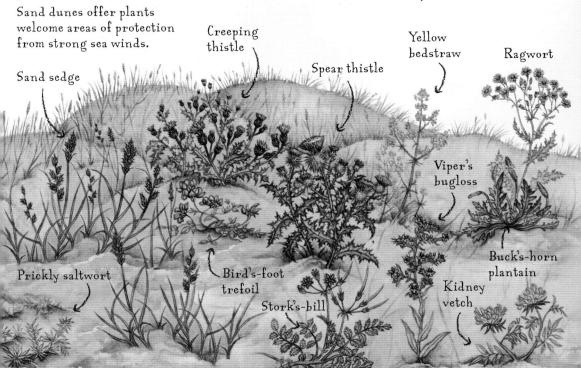

Sand sedge

Creeping thistle

Spear thistle

Yellow bedstraw

Ragwort

Viper's bugloss

Prickly saltwort

Bird's-foot trefoil

Stork's-bill

Kidney vetch

Buck's-horn plantain

Sea cliffs

From a distance, towering sea cliffs often look barren, which is hardly surprising, as conditions there are so hostile. Plants that dare to grow are constantly buffeted by gales and lashed with salty sea spray, which draws fresh water out of them. When it rains, it often pours. But even on the flat ledges and clifftops, the rainwater trickles quickly away between the rocks.

Flowers that thrive often have deep, wide-spreading roots, which hold them fast and reach into cracks and crevices where rainwater collects.

Without long roots to anchor them, these three tall, clifftop flowers would soon be blown away.

Golden rod

Red valerian

Wild cabbage

Many plants grow low, to keep out of the wind. A few sprout from nooks on perilous ledges, but you'll find most flowers peppering the wiry grass on clifftops, where there's more soil.

Here are some of the plants that grow on cliffs.

WARNING
Some flowers are well designed for clinging to steep cliffs, but people aren't. So always keep away from the edge.

Sea campion

Rock samphire

Wild cabbage

Thrift

Rock sea spurrey

Sea kale

Salt marshes

Salt marshes are found in low-lying areas near the coast. Regular flooding by high tides turns the land into a boggy mixture of mud, sand and salt water. Some plants have developed specialized ways to survive in these salty surroundings.

Sea lavender, for example, stores excess salt in bumps on its leaves, which burst to release the salt. Annual seablite can store fresh water in its fleshy leaves.

Areas close to the sea are flooded twice a day. This is just too much salt and water for many plants, so you'll find more varieties growing on parts of the marshes that are further away from the sea.

Look for these flowers on the upper salt marshes, beyond the reach of the usual daily tides.

These salt-marsh plants can cope with frequent washings of salty water, so they grow near to the sea.

Annual seablite

Sea arrow grass

WARNING

Take care when you walk on salt marshes as it's easy to sink into the mud. Go with a friend and wear rubber boots.

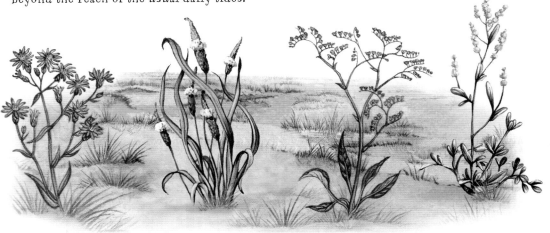

Sea aster   Sea plantain   Sea lavender   Sea purslane

Moors and heaths

Moors and heaths are wide open areas of land that are usually swept by wind. Some are very dry, but in others, frequent heavy rain clogs up the soil and washes nutrients away. You'll find fewer flowers on moors and heaths than in meadows and fields. But the ones that do grow, such as heather and gorse, sometimes take over large areas.

Here are some plants that can grow low to survive the windy conditions on heaths and moorland.

Here are some of the flowers you can find on moors and heaths.

Gorse

Sheep's bit

Bell heather

Gorse

Bell heather

Sundew

Sheep's bit

Marshes

Marshes are open, grassy areas that are waterlogged for some or all of the year – a bit like wet meadows. The ground is often so full of water that there isn't much air for the roots to breathe. Marsh plants often have tiny pockets of air inside their leaves and stems. This air can be pumped to the roots to stop them from drowning.

These common flowers thrive in bogs and marshes.

Meadowsweet

Many marsh plants, like these, have large leaves, so the plants can lose excess water through them.

Great willowherb

Water avens

Marsh marigold

Marsh violet

Common meadowrue

Ragged Robin

Harebell

Bilberry

In the mountains

How many types of
mountain flowers
can you spot here?

Freezing temperatures, cruel winds, dry ground and poor soil make mountains the ultimate endurance challenge. The higher up you go, the fewer flowers you'll find. A number of species have learned to survive, though, and in spring, brighten the bleak landscape with flowers.

Strong winds can uproot flowers, so they have to grow long roots over a wide area to grip the ground. Some roots even work their way into cracks in rocks for extra security. Many mountain flowers grow in low, thick mats, which leave less of the plant exposed to the howling wind.

Helpful leaves

All plants lose water through their leaves and many mountain plants have small leaves, to avoid losing too much. Some are hairy too, to keep them warm and catch water droplets.

These mountain flowers have all found ways to survive the harsh conditions.

Common butterwort

Alpine forget-me-not

Alpine milk vetch

Opposite-leaved golden saxifrage

Alpine Lady's mantle

Alpine rock cress

Starry saxifrage

Moss campion

Alpine fleabane

Wild flowers to spot

In this section of the book, you'll find pictures and descriptions of wild flowers to spot. They tell you where and when to look, as well as useful facts about their height or length and distinctive features. The flowers are grouped by colour.

You can find links to more flower identification guides on the Usborne Quicklinks Website at *www.usborne-quicklinks.com*

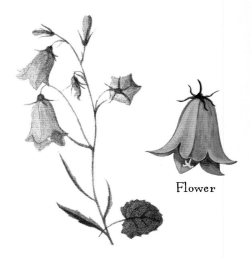
Flower

Harebell

10–25cm (4–10in). Flowers divided into five lobes. Rounded leaves in a rosette at base of stem. Grassland, moors and gardens. July–September.

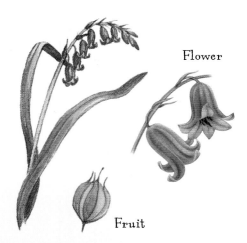
Flower

Fruit

Bluebell

30cm (12in). Also called wild hyacinth. Clusters of flowers. Shiny leaves. Grows in thick carpets in woods. April–May.

Bud

Viper's bugloss

30cm (12in). Pink buds become blue flowers. Long, narrow leaves on rough, bristly stems. Roadsides and sand dunes. June–September.

214

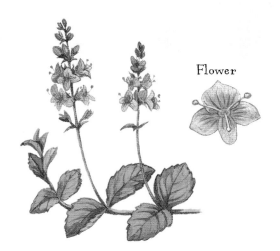

Flower

Heath speedwell

30cm (12in). Flowers grow in upright spikes. Hairy, oval leaves. Grows close to the ground in grassy places and woods. May–August.

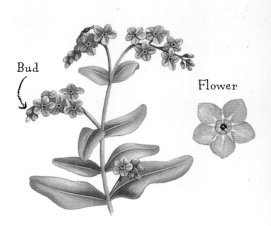

Bud

Flower

Forget-me-not

20cm (8in). Pink buds become tiny, blue flowers. Furry leaves. Open places, farmland and gardens. April–October.

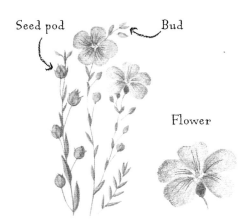

Seed pod   Bud

Flower

Blue flax

30–100cm (12–39in). Flowers have silky petals. Narrow, spear-shaped leaves. Meadows and roadsides. June–August.

Bud

Chicory

30–120cm (12–47in). Flowers are usually blue or, very rarely, pink or white. Waste ground, roadsides and hedgerows. July–October.

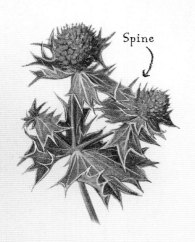

Sea holly

20–60cm (8–24in). Flowers packed
closely together in round flower
heads. Spine-tipped leaves. Sandy
and pebbly beaches. July–August.

Common milkwort

5–35cm (2–14in). Clusters of flowers
that can be blue, pink, lilac or white.
Grassy places and sand dunes.
May–September.

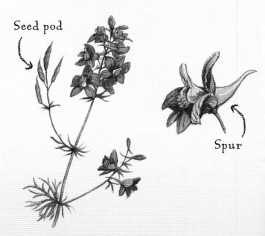

Cornflower

40cm (16in). Scaly leaf-like
structures beneath cluster of
flowers. Cornfields, waste ground
and gardens. July–August.

Larkspur

50cm (20in). Spikes of purple, pink
or white flowers. A spur sticks out
behind each flower. Feathery
leaves. Waste ground. June–July.

WILD FLOWERS TO SPOT

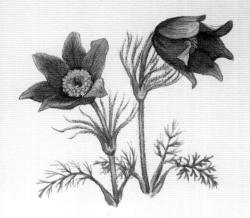

Pasque flower

10cm (4in). Purple or white bell-shaped flowers. Silky petals and stem. Deeply divided leaves. Gardens, rare in meadows. April–May.

Snake's head fritillary

10cm (4in). Rare in Europe. Can be pinkish-purple and checked, or white with faint pink or green veins. Damp meadows and woods. March–May.

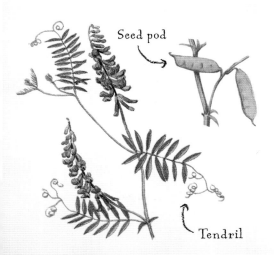

Seed pod

Tendril

Flower

Tufted vetch

50cm–200cm (20–79in). Climbing plant with curly, leaf-like tendrils. Hedges, roadsides and woods. June–September.

Foxglove

150cm (59in). Spotted, trumpet-shaped flowers that usually grow on only one side of the stem. Woods and grassy banks. June–September.

Flower

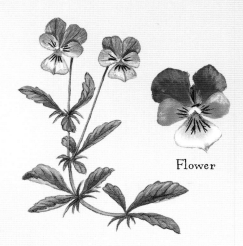

Flower

Cuckoo flower

15–50cm (6–20in). Flowers are pale lilac, sometimes white. Wet meadows, marshes and hedgerows. April–June.

Wild pansy

15cm (6in). Bright flowers that are often three-coloured. Oval leaves. Farmland, waste ground and gardens. April–October.

Fruit

Bloody crane's-bill

30cm (12in). Also known as blood-red geranium. Bright, pinkish-purple flowers. Hairy stem. Cliffs and meadows. June–August.

Common dog violet

10cm (4in). Creeping plant with rosettes of heart-shaped leaves and pointed sepals. Woods and hedges. March–June.

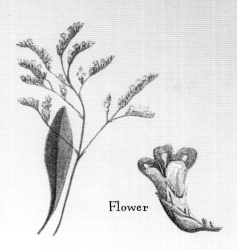

Flower

Flower

Flower

Sea lavender

20–50cm (8–20in). Purple flowers with yellow anthers. Slender, wiry stems. Salt marshes, often grows in large clumps. July–September.

Marsh violet

5–50cm (2–20in). Lilac flowers with dark purple veins. Heart-shaped or kidney-shaped leaves. Marshes. April–July.

Columbine

30–100cm (12–39in). Flowers are usually purple or blue, but can be pink or white. Wet meadows, open woodland and hedgerows. May–July.

Early purple orchid

60cm (24in). Flowers usually purple, but sometimes pink or white. Purple-tinged stem. Dark spots on leaves. Woods and hedges. April–July.

Seed pod

Common poppy

60cm (24in). Upright plant with stiff hairs on stem. Round seed pods grow in late summer. Cornfields and waste ground. June–August.

Sweet William

60cm (24in). Flat cluster of flowers. Pink or mauve petals with a spicy scent. Farmland, roadsides and mountains. May–June.

Flower

Unripe fruit

Scarlet pimpernel

15cm (6in). Creeping plant. Blue flowers sometimes found growing alongside the more usual red ones. Farmland. June–August.

Sorrel

20–100cm (8–40in). Also known as spinach dock. Clusters of tiny flowers. Grows in large patches in meadows. May–July.

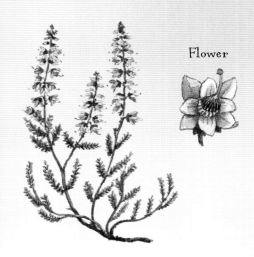

Flower

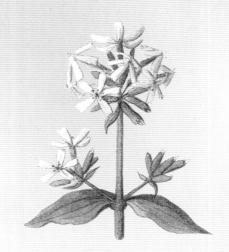

Heather

20cm (8in). Also known as ling. Tiny, pink or white flowers. Overlapping leaves. Grows in carpets on moors. July–September.

Soapwort

30–100cm (12–39in). Flowers are pale pink, sometimes white. Pale leaves with three veins. Waste ground, hedgerows and roadsides. May–September.

Flower

Seed pod

Great willowherb

100–200cm (39–79in). Flowers usually pink, occasionally white. Hairy leaves and stems. By rivers and streams, and in damp meadows. June–September.

Red campion

60cm (24in). Dark pink flowers. Also comes in white and pale pink varieties. Hairy leaves and stem. Woods. May–June.

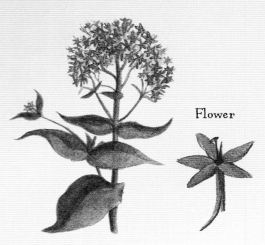

Flower

Ragged Robin

30–70cm (12–28in). Bright pink, raggedy petals. Also comes in white. Marshes and damp meadows. May–July.

Red valerian

30–80cm (12–32in). Flowers can be red, pink or white. Coastal rocks and cliffs, old walls, sandy places. May–September.

Seed pod

Flower

Herb Robert

40cm (16in). Flowers have a strong, unpleasant smell. Hairy leaves and stem that turn red in autumn. Woods and hedges. May–September.

Rest harrow

10–70cm (4–28in). Flowers can be pink or purple. Leaves covered with sticky hairs. Dry, grassy places and sand dunes. June–September.

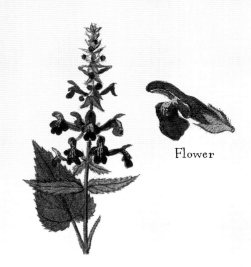

Flower

Wood woundwort

50–120cm (20–47in). Toothed leaves that give off a strong, unpleasant smell. Woods, hedgerows and roadsides. July–September.

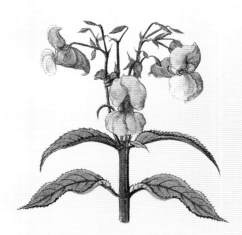

Policeman's helmet

100–200cm (39–79in). Flowers can be pink, purple or white. Leaves are edged with red teeth. By rivers and streams. July–October.

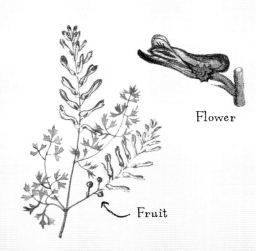

Flower

Fruit

Fumitory

20–100cm (8–39in). Grey-green leaves. Small, round fruit. Waste ground, roadsides and hedgerows. March–November.

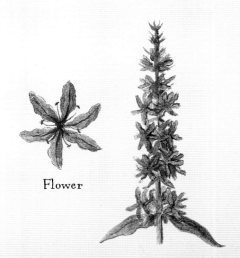

Flower

Flower

Purple loosestrife

50–180cm (20–71in). Hairy stem and leaves. Grows in clumps on marshes, and by streams and rivers. June–September.

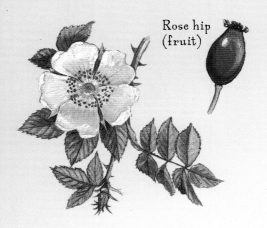

Rose hip
(fruit)

Dog rose

3m (10ft). Sweet-scented, pink or white flowers. Thorny stems. Shiny, red, fruits develop in autumn. Hedges and woods. June–July.

Snowdrop

20cm (8in). Drooping flowers with honey-like scent. Slender stem and long, flat leaves. Comes in several varieties. Woods. January–March.

Bud

Greater bindweed

3m (10ft). Climbing plant. Large, white flowers, sometimes with pale pink stripes. Hedges and riverbanks. July–September.

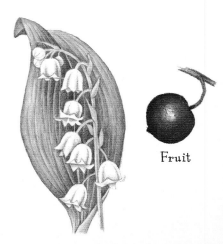

Fruit

Lily-of-the-valley

20cm (8in). Sweet-smelling flowers. Two wide, shiny, leathery leaves. Bright orange-red berries in summer. Woods and gardens. May–June.

Fruit

Fruit

Goosegrass

60cm (24in). Climbing plant. Tiny, white flowers. Leaves, stem and fruit covered with hooked bristles. Hedges. June–September.

Blackberry

3m (10ft). Also known as bramble. Sharp prickles on stems and under leaves. Berries grow in autumn. Hedges and woods. June–September.

Flower

Wood anemone

15cm (6in). Also called granny's nightcap. Petals are white with pink streaks on the outside. Grows in large patches in woods. March–June.

Yarrow

60cm (24in). Flat-topped clusters of white or pink flowers. Rough stem and feathery leaves. Hedges and meadows. June–August.

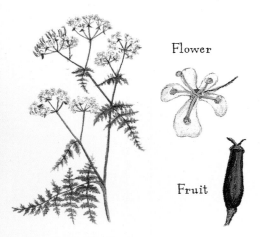

Flower

Fruit

Closed
flower
head

Cow parsley

100cm (40in). Also called Lady's lace.
Clusters of tiny flowers. Ribbed stem
and feathery leaves. Hedge banks,
roadsides and ditches. May–June.

Oxeye daisy

60cm (24in). Flowers close at night.
Large leaves at base of stem, smaller
leaves further up. Gardens and
waste ground. June–August.

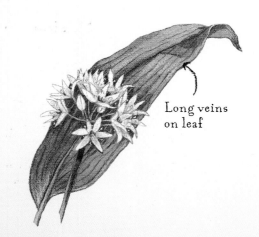

Long veins
on leaf

Ramsons

10–25cm (4–10in). Also known as
wild garlic. Flowers have strong,
garlicky smell. Long, shiny leaves.
Damp, shady woods. April–June.

Scented mayweed

60cm (24in). A fast-growing plant
with feathery leaves and an apple-
like scent. Farmland and waste
ground. June–July.

Closed
flower
head

Daisy

10cm (4in). Rosette of leaves at base of stem. Flowers close at night and in bad weather. Most grassy places. January–October.

White dead-nettle

60cm (24in). White or greenish-white lipped flowers. Hairy leaves that don't sting. Hedges and waste ground. March–November.

Four-leaf
clover

White clover

10–25cm (4–10in). Dense flower heads that are usually white or pale pink. Leaves have a white band. Parks, gardens and meadows. April–August.

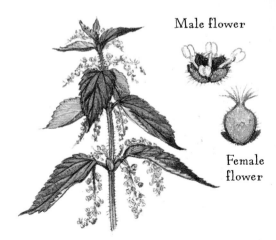

Male flower

Female
flower

Stinging nettle

100cm (40in). Leaves and stem covered with stinging hairs. Damp, shady spots, and woods by streams and rivers. June–August.

Flower

Lady's bedstraw

10–80cm (4–32in). Honey-scented flowers. Shiny leaves, hairy underneath. Dry, grassy places and sand dunes. May–September.

Creeping buttercup

10–50cm (4–20in). Shiny flowers. Long, trailing stems and hairy leaves. Grows close to the ground in grassy places. May–August.

Bud

Marsh marigold

10–45cm (4–18in). Shiny, saucer-shaped flowers. Toothed, heart-shaped leaves. Marshes and wet meadows. March–June.

Bud

Primrose

15cm (6in). Often first flower of spring. Soft, wrinkled leaves and hairy stems. Grows in patches in woods, hedges and fields. December–May.

St. John's wort

60cm (24in). Clusters of deep yellow flowers with many stamens. Black dots on anthers. Damp, grassy places. June–September.

Silverweed

10–30cm (4–12in). Leaves densely hairy underneath. Red runners. Grassland, roadsides and waste ground. May–September.

Bud

Common rockrose

10–40cm (4–16in). Flowers can be yellow, cream or orange. Leaves are hairy underneath. Grassland and rocky ground. May–September.

Sepals

Cowslip

15cm (6in). Golden-yellow flowers with long sepals. Rosette of long, crinkled leaves at base of stem. Meadows. April–May.

Fruit

Dandelion

15cm (6in). Square-tipped, yellow petals. Rosette of toothed leaves. Hairy, white seed head. Grassy areas and roadsides. March–June.

Monkey flower

10–50cm (8–20in). Bright yellow flowers with red spots. Square stems. Marshes, river banks and by streams. June–September.

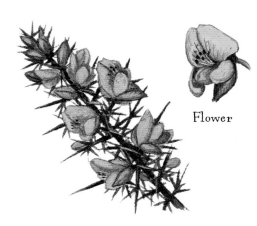

Flower

Ragwort

30–150cm (12–59in). Yellow flower heads. Fruits have "parachutes" of white hairs. Grassland and sand dunes. June-September.

Gorse

1–2m (40–80in). Also known as furze. Flowers smell like coconut and vanilla. Dark-green, spiny leaves. Moors and waste ground. March–June.

Seed pod

Fruit

Bird's-foot trefoil

10cm (4in). Also known as bacon and eggs. Creeping plant. Flowers are yellow with red streaks. Grassy banks. May–June.

Snapdragon

40cm (16in). Flowers come in lots of different colours, including purple, yellow and white. Gardens, rocks and old walls. June–September.

Flower

Kidney vetch

10–60cm (4–24in). Flowers can be yellow, orange or sometimes red. Thick, hairy sepals. Grassland, rocks and sand dunes. May–September.

Yellow rattle

10–50cm (4–20in). Yellow flowers with violet tips. Toothed leaves. Fruits are seed pods. Grassland and roadsides. May–July.

Glossary

Here are some words in the book you might not know. Any word in *italics* is defined elsewhere in the glossary.

anther The blobby tip of a *stamen*, where *pollen* is made.

bud An undeveloped flower or leaf.

bulb A thick, underground stem, covered in scaly leaves, which a plant uses to store food and produce new plants.

canopy The layer formed by the leaves and branches of trees in a wood.

climbing plant A plant that grows upwards using a wall, fence or other plant for support.

corm A short, swollen underground stem, which a plant uses to store food and produce new plants.

creeping plant A plant that grows along the ground.

field A large area of land, often used for growing crops and keeping animals.

fruit Part of a plant that holds its *seeds*.

heath An open area of windy, well-drained land.

leaflet A single part of a divided leaf that is made up of several separate sections.

lobed leaf A type of leaf or *leaflet*, partly divided into sections called lobes.

marsh An open, grassy area that is waterlogged for some or all of the year.

meadow A large area of land used for growing grasses to make hay.

moor An open area of land that is wet and windy.

nectar A sweet liquid made near the bases of petals to attract insects which will move *pollen* to another flower of the same type.

nutrients Chemicals that a plant needs for growth.

ovary The lower part of the *pistil* that contains *ovules*.

ovule A plant's "egg", which combines with a grain of *pollen* to make a *seed*.

petals Parts of a flower that surround the *pistil* and *stamens*. Petals are often brightly coloured.

pistil A female part of a flower. See also *stigma* and *ovary*.

pollen A powder made by a flower's male parts for transfer to the female parts to make *seeds*.

rhizome An underground stem that grows horizontally, and produces roots and leaves, which can develop into new plants.

root A part of a plant that anchors it into the ground, and absorbs water and *nutrients* from the soil.

rosette A circle of leaves growing from a single point.

runner A stem that grows along the ground, putting down roots that can grow into new plants.

salt marsh A low-lying coastal area, where the land is regularly flooded by sea water.

sand dune A large ridge of wind-blown sand.

seed A fertilized *ovule* that may grow into a new plant.

seedling A very young plant, that has grown from a *seed*.

seed pod A tough, dry *fruit*.

sepals Leaf-like parts that protect a flower while it is a *bud*.

spur A narrow, hollow cone at the base of a *petal* that sticks out behind a flower.

stamen The male part of a flower, where *pollen* is made. See also *anther*.

stigma The sticky tip of a *pistil*, to which *pollen* attaches.

tendril A slender leaf or stem, which twines around objects for support.

toothed leaf A leaf or *leaflet* with jagged edges.

weed Any plant growing where it is not wanted.

Poppies and buttercups in a meadow

Index

Acknowledgements

Every effort has been made to trace the copyright holders of material in this book. If any rights have been omitted, the publishers offer to rectify this in any subsequent editions following notification. The publishers are grateful to the following organisations and individuals for their permission to reproduce material

(t = top, m = middle, b = bottom, l = left, r = right):

Cover © The Photolibrary Wales/Alamy, © Sindre Ellingsen/Alamy, © David Kjaer/naturepl.com; **p2-3** © Jeremy Pardoe/Alamy; **p4-5** © David Noton/naturepl.com; **p6-7** © Andrew Darrington/Alamy; **p11** © Michael Quinton/Minden Pictures/FLPA; **p12** © Mark Hamblin (rspb-images.com); **p18** © NHPA/STEPHEN DALTON; **p19** © NHPA/WILLIAM PATON; **p20** © Warren Photographic; **p26** © Terry Andrewartha/naturepl.com; **p28** (tl) © Frank Lane Picture Agency/CORBIS, (b) © George Reszeter, Ardea London Ltd; **p30** © Warren Photographic; **p31** © Bob Glover (rspb-images.com); **p32** © Warren Photographic; **p33** © Kim Taylor/naturepl.com; **p34** © NHPA/MANFRED DANEGGER; **p36** © Mike Read (rspb-images.com); **p37** © Warren Photographic; **p42** © Georgette Douwma/naturepl.com; **p44** © John Daniels, Ardea London Ltd; **p45** © STOCKPHOTO/Alamy; **p46** © Duncan Usher, Ardea London Ltd; **p48** © NHPA/ALAN WILLIAMS; **p49** © Worldwide Picture Library/Alamy; **p52** © STUART ANTHONY SILVER; **p53** © van hilversum/Alamy; **p55** © Kim Taylor/naturepl.com; **p62** © Wayne Hutchinson/FLPA; **p68** © Steve Packham/naturepl.com; **p69** © Solvin Zankl/naturepl.com; **p72** © Gary K Smith/FLPA; **p74** © Dietmar Nill/naturepl.com; **p76** © Jorma Luhta/naturepl.com.; **p80-81** © blickwinkel/Alamy; **p82-83** © tim gartside/Alamy; **p84-85** © Digital Vision; **p86** © PCL/Alamy; **p88** © Royalty-Free/Corbis; **p91** © Nigel Cattlin/FLPA; **p95** © Wegner/ARCO/naturepl.com; **p97** © Digital Vision; **p99** © Owen Franken/CORBIS; **p101** © Cambridge2000.com; **p103** © Christopher Barnes/Alamy; **p104** © Den Reader/Alamy; **p108** © Jan Vermeer/Foto Natura/FLPA; **p111** © Brand X Pictures/Alamy; **p112** © Michael Marten/Science Photo Library; **p115** © Aflo/Naturepl.com; **p117** © artpartner-images.com/Alamy; **p121** © Michael Piazza/OSF; **p122** © Duncan Usher/Ardea London Ltd; **p124** © Photowood Inc./CORBIS; **p127** © NHPA/Alan Williams; **p130** © Lothar Lenz/zefa/Corbis; **p133** © Leroy Simon/Visuals Unlimited/Getty Images; **p134** © imagebroker/Alamy; **p136** © blickwinkel/Alamy; **p139** © Marc Grimberg/Alamy; **p140** © Digital Vision; **p141** © Digital Vision; **p142** © Bloom Works Inc./Alamy; **p143** © Keith Douglas/Alamy; **p157** © Organics image library/Alamy; **p158-159** © Bob Gibbons/ardea.com; **p160-161** © David Kjaer/naturepl.com; **p163** © Chris Gomersall/naturepl.com; **p18** © Rolf Kopfle, Ardea London Ltd; **p174** © South West Images Scotland/Alamy; **p176** © Dougal Waters/Photodisk Red/Getty Images; **p179** © Richard Taylor-Jones/Alamy; **p180** © Bob Gibbons/Science Photo Library; **p183** © Beata Moore/Alamy; **p185** © blickwinkel/Alamy; **p186** © ImageState/Alamy; **p189** © Tony Wharton/FLPA; **p190** © David Chapman/Alamy; **p193** © Ingram Publishing/Alamy; **p200-201** © Joe Mamer Photography/Alamy; **p202-203** © Dietrich Rose/zefa/Corbis; **p232-233** © ImageState/Alamy

Written by Susanna Davidson, Sarah Courtauld, Kate Davies, Laura Howell, Sarah Khan and Kirsteen Rogers

Designed by Helen Wood, Non Figg, Laura Parker, Laura Hammonds, Reuben Barrance, Michael Hill, Kate Rimmer, Marc Maynard and Nayera Everall

Additional designs by Hannah Ahmed and Stella Baggot, Brenda Cole, Joanne Kirkby and Tom Lalonde

Digital manipulation by Will Dawes, Keith Furnival, John Russell and Nick Wakeford

Additional editorial contributions by Hazel Maskell and Rachel Firth

Edited by Jane Chisholm

Additional illustrators: Dave Ashby, Mike Atkinson, Graham Austin, Bob Bampton, John Barber, Amanda Barlow, David Baxter, Andrew Beckett, Joyce Bee, Stephen Bennett, Roland Berry, Isabel Bowring, Trevor Boyer, Wendy Bramall, Maggie Brand, Paul Brooks, Peter Bull, Mark Burgess, Hilary Burn, Liz Butler, Terry Callcut, Sue Camm, Lynn Chadwick, Kuo Kang Chen, Roger H Coggins, Frankie Coventry, Patrick Cox, Christine Darter, Kate Davies, Sarah De Ath, Kevin Dean, Peter Dennis, Brin Edwards, Michelle Emblem, Sandra Fernandez, Denise Finney, Don Forrest, Sarah Fox-Davies, John Francis, Nigel Frey, Sheila Galbraith, William Giles, Victoria Gooman, Victoria Gordon, Teri Gower, Coral Guppy, Laura Hammonds, Alan Harris, Nick Harris, Tim Hayward, Bob Hersey, Chris Howell-Jones, Christine Howes, David Hurrell, Ian Jackson, Ian McNee, Roger Kent, Aziz Khan, Colin King, Deborah King, Steven Kirk, Jonathan Langley, Richard Lewington, Ken Lily, Mick Loates, Rachel Lockwood, Kevin Lyles, Chris Lyon, Alan Male, Alan Marks, Andy Martin, Josephine Martin, Rodney Matthews, Uwe Mayer, Rob McCaig, Joseph McEwan, Malcolm McGregor, Doreen McGuinness, Caroline McLean, Dee McLean, Richard Millington, Annabel Milne, David More, Dee Morgan, Robert Morton, Patricia Mynott, David Nash, Tricia Newell, Barbara Nicholson, Richard Orr, David Palmer, Charles Pearson, Liz Pepperell, Julie Piper, Gillian Platt, Maurice Pledger, Cynthia Pow, Mike Pringle, David Quinn, Charles Raymond, Barry Raynor, Phillip Richardson, Jim Robbins, Peter Scott, John Shackell, Chris Shields, Maggie Silver, Gwen Simpson, Guy Smith, Annabel Spenceley, Peter Stebbing, Ralph Stobart, Sue Testar, George Thompson, Joan Thompson, Joyce Tuhill, Sally Volke, Peter Warner, David Watson, Phil Weare, Adrian Williams, Roy Wiltshire, James Woods, David Wright, John Yates